The LITTLE BLACK SONGBOOK

COLDPLAY

Wise Publications
part of The Music Sales Group
London / New York / Paris / Sydney / Copenhagen / Berlin / Madrid / Tokyo

Published by
Wise Publications
14-15 Berners Street, London, W1T 3LJ, UK.
Exclusive distributors:
Music Sales Limited
Distribution Centre,
Newmarket Road, Bury St Edmunds, Suffolk, IP33 3YB, UK.
Music Sales Pty Limited
120 Rothschild Avenue, Rosebery, NSW 2018, Australia.

Order No. AM989912
ISBN 13: 978-1-84772-013-9

Music arranged by Martin Shellard.
Cover photograph Steven Dewall/Retna.
Printed in China.

www.musicsales.com

Relative Tuning

The guitar can be tuned with the aid of pitch pipes or dedicated electronic guitar tuners which are available through your local music dealer. If you do not have a tuning device, you can use relative tuning. Estimate the pitch of the 6th string as near as possible to E or at least a comfortable pitch (not too high, as you might break other strings in tuning up). Then, while checking the various positions on the diagram, place a finger from your left hand on the:

5th fret of the E or 6th string and **tune the open A** (or 5th string) to the note (A)

5th fret of the A or 5th string and **tune the open D** (or 4th string) to the note (D)

5th fret of the D or 4th string and **tune the open G** (or 3rd string) to the note (G)

4th fret of the G or 3rd string and **tune the open B** (or 2nd string) to the note (B)

5th fret of the B or 2nd string and **tune the open E** (or 1st string) to the note (E)

Reading Chord Boxes

Chord boxes are diagrams of the guitar neck viewed head upwards, face on as illustrated. The top horizontal line is the nut, unless a higher fret number is indicated, the others are the frets.

The vertical lines are the strings, starting from E (or 6th) on the left to E (or 1st) on the right.

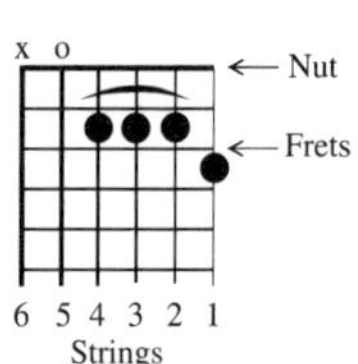

The black dots indicate where to place your fingers.

Strings marked with an O are played open, not fretted. Strings marked with an X should not be played.

The curved bracket indicates a 'barre' - hold down the strings under the bracket with your first finger, using your other fingers to fret the remaining notes.

1.36

Words & Music by
Guy Berryman, Jon Buckland, Will Champion & Chris Martin

Em/G E5 G6 F♯11 B7 B7sus4

Capo first fret

Intro

| Em/G E5 | Em/G E5 |
| Em/G E5 | Em/G E5 ‖

Verse 1

```
Em/G E5
Stuck in a corner
        Em/G E5
Are mon - keys in cages
        Em/G E5
That don't have a number
     Em/G E5
To fight one another.
G6  F♯6add11
       Try to recover.

| Em/G   E5       | Em/G   E5       |

Em/G  E5
Climb up the ladder
         Em/G  E5
Look up     and you see birds
Em/G E5
Blind as each other.
        Em/G E5
How long can we suffer?
G6              F♯11
   We're as blind as each other.

| Em/G   E5       | Em/G   E5       |
| Em/G   E5       | Em/G   E5       |
```

Chorus 1

```
B7          B7sus4
   On the cloud that you sit in
B7                B7sus4
   There's one born every minute
B7     B7sus4
   So much to discover,
B7       B7sus4
   I've become a believer.

| Em/G   E5            | Em/G   E5            |
| Em/G   E5            | Em/G   E5            |
```

Verse 2

```
Em/G E5
Sis  -  ters and brothers,
     Em/G E5
Who fight one another
      Em/G  E5
Will mourn and deceive us,
     Em/G E5
Will find  us and keep us.
G6  F♯11
    Take us or leave us.

| Em/G   E5            | Em/G   E5            |

Em/G E5
How soon is now? Yeah.
Em/G E5
How long is never?
     Em/G E5
I'm no  -  thing but normal
       Em/G   E5
With some - thing together.
G6         F♯11
   Come on, stick together.

| Em/G   E5            | Em/G   E5            |
| Em/G   E5            | Em/G   E5            |
```

Chorus 2

```
B7          B7sus4
   On the cloud that you sit in
B7                B7sus4
   There's one born every minute
B7    B7sus4
   So much to discover,
B7      B7sus4
   I've become a believer.
```

Outro

```
| Em/G   E5          | Em/G   E5          |
| Em/G   E5          | Em/G   E5          |
| Em/G   E5          | Em/G   E5          |
| Em/G   E5          | Em/G   E5          |
| G6                 | F#11     N.C.      ||
```

AMSTERDAM

Words & Music by
Guy Berryman, Jon Buckland, Will Champion & Chris Martin

D A Esus4 G E Gmaj7 Eadd9 G6

Capo first fret

```
Intro    | D    A    | Esus4  E  G | D    A    | Esus4  E  G |
         | D    A    | Esus4  E  G | D    A    | E     G(fermata) ||

Verse 1  D              A      Esus4  E       G
           Come on,   oh my        star is fading,
         D         A              Esus4  E       G
           And I    swerve out       of control.
         D         A     Esus4 E   G
           If I'd,    if I'd      only waited,
         D                A                       E       G
           I'd not be stuck here in this      hole. —

Link 1   | D    A    | Esus4  E  G | D    A    | Esus4  E  G |

Verse 2  D                A      Esus4  E       G
           Come here,   oh my        star is fading,
         D         A              Esus4  E       G
           And I    swerve out       of control
         D         A              Esus4  E       G
           And I    swear, I wait  -  ed and waited.
         D                A                      E       G
           I've got to get out of this      hole. —

Chorus 1      Eadd9                     Gmaj7
         But time is on your side,
                           D        A
         It's on your side     now.
                                Eadd9
         Not pushing you down,
                      Gmaj7
         And all around
                   D                      A
         It's no cause for concern.
```

Instrumental 1 | D A | Esus4 E G | D A | Esus4 E G |

| D A | Esus4 E G | D A | E G(fermata) ||

```
        D            A     Esus4 E     G
Verse 3   Come on,    oh my     star is fading,
        D         A          Esus4  E    G
          And I    see no chance of release.
        D         A            Esus4  E     G
          And I know I'm dead    on the surface
        D            A            Esus4 E       Gmaj7
          But I am screaming under-neath. —
```

```
              Eadd9                     Gmaj7
Chorus 2  And time is on your side,
                               D        A
          It's on your side     now.
                                Eadd9
          Not pushing you down,
                        Gmaj7
          And all around
                      D                  A
          No it's no cause for concern.
```

Instrumental 2 | Eadd9 | Gmaj7 G6 | D | A |

| Eadd9 | Gmaj7 G6 | D ||

```
          A                        Eadd9                    Gmaj7
Chorus 3    Stuck on the end    of this ball and chain
                                     D            A
          And I'm on my way    back down,    yeah.
                                    Eadd9                Gmaj7
          Stood on the edge,    tied to the noose,
                              D       A
          Sick to the stomach.
                                                Eadd9
          You can say what you mean,
                                               Gmaj7
          But it won't change a thing.
```

cont.

```
                  D     A
I'm sick of our se - crets.
                  Eadd9             Gmaj7
Stood on the edge,   tied to the noose
                    D                         A    Eadd9
And you came along,   and you cut me loose.
Gmaj7             D                         A    Eadd9
  You came along    and you cut me loose.
Gmaj7             D                         A (fermata)
  You came along    and you cut me loose.
```

ANIMALS

Words & Music by
Guy Berryman, Jon Buckland, Will Champion & Chris Martin

Cmaj7 D6/9 E G6 Am6

Capo third fret

Intro ||: Cmaj7 | D6/9 | Cmaj7 | D6/9 :||

Verse 1
```
E                 G6
Animals we are
   Cmaj7        Am6              E
Disposable, collapsible and raw
        G6
In you go
  Cmaj7              Am6
Into some crowded room
     E      G6
And animals climb
              Cmaj7           Am6               E
And they're climbing over you until you say,
              G6            Cmaj7   Am6
"Off you go, off you go."
```

Link 1 ||: E G6 | Cmaj7 Am6 :||

Verse 2
```
E             G6
Animal I am,
          Cmaj7               Am6        E
And I'm looking for an answer just like you
               G6            Cmaj7     Am6
And I should know which way to turn.
   E           G6
An animal that runs
       Cmaj7          Am6            E
And I ran away from you because I'm scared
                G6           Cmaj7   Am6
Now off you go, off you go.
```

Chorus 1

```
Cmaj7                              D%
   And if you're gonna go, go now,
Cmaj7                              D%
   And if you're gonna go, go now
Cmaj7                         D%
   And I forgot to tell you how
Cmaj7                    D%
   So if you're gonna go . . . go (now).
```

Link 2

```
||: E        G6        | Cmaj7    Am6   :||
  now.
```

Verse 3

```
E              G6
Animal you are,
    Cmaj7       Am6
Disposable, defenceless, yes and
E                G6               Cmaj7         Am6
   Watch your mouth  boys, watch your mouth.
    E             G6
An animal that runs
        Cmaj7              Am6
And I made all my excuses to you
E                        G6            Cmaj7       Am6
   And I missed my chance by a stone's throw.
```

Chorus 2

```
Cmaj7                              D%
   And if you're gonna go, go now,
Cmaj7                              D%
   And if you're gonna go, go now
Cmaj7                         D%
   And I forgot to tell you how
Cmaj7                         D%
   So if you're gonna go . . .    go . . .
```

Link 3

```
                                              x4
||: E        G6           | Cmaj7    Am6      :||
  now.                                       (go)
```

Outro

```
       E          G6
And I crumble, crumble and fall
Cmaj7                      Am6
Crumble and fall like an animal
  E          G6
I crumble, crumble and fall
Cmaj7                      Am6
Crumble and fall like an animal
```

cont.

```
        E          G6
Yes I crumble, crumble and fall
Cmaj7                      Am6
Crumble and fall like an animal
        E          G6
Yes I crumble, crumble and fall
Cmaj7                      Am6
Crumble and fall like an animal.
```

```
‖: E       G6          | Cmaj7    Am6        :‖
```

Repeat ad lib to finish

BIGGER STRONGER

Words & Music by
Guy Berryman, Jon Buckland, Will Champion & Chris Martin

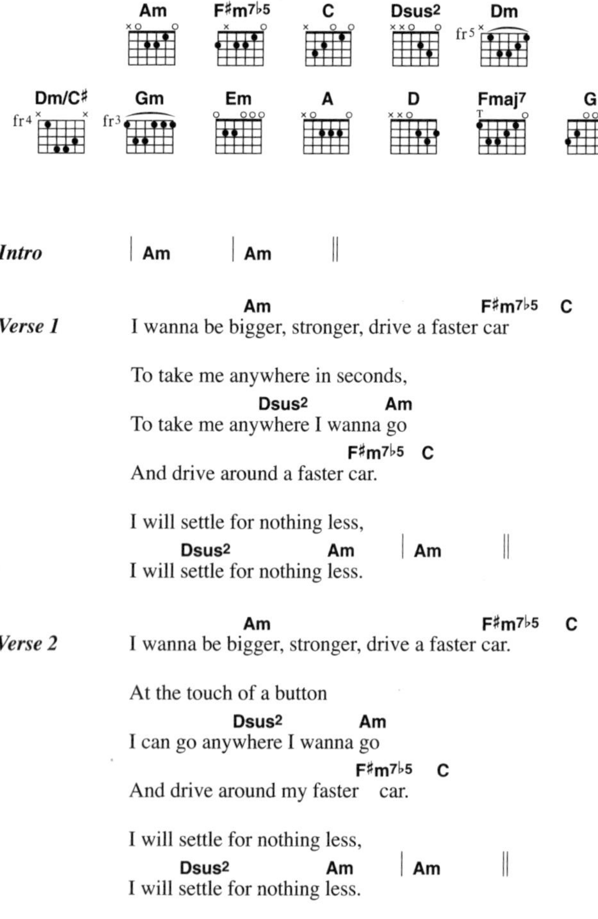

Intro | Am | Am ||

Verse 1

Am F♯m7♭5 C
I wanna be bigger, stronger, drive a faster car

To take me anywhere in seconds,
Dsus2 Am
To take me anywhere I wanna go
F♯m7♭5 C
And drive around a faster car.

I will settle for nothing less,
Dsus2 Am | Am ||
I will settle for nothing less.

Verse 2

Am F♯m7♭5 C
I wanna be bigger, stronger, drive a faster car.

At the touch of a button
Dsus2 Am
I can go anywhere I wanna go
F♯m7♭5 C
And drive around my faster car.

I will settle for nothing less,
Dsus2 Am | Am ||
I will settle for nothing less.

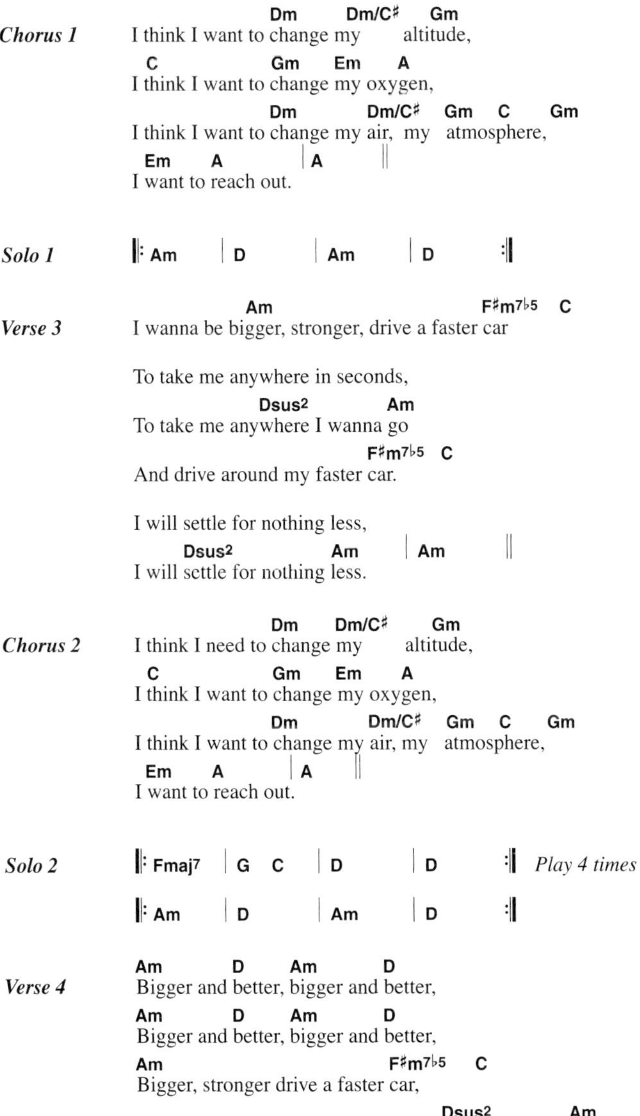
Chorus 1
Dm Dm/C♯ Gm
I think I want to change my altitude,
C Gm Em A
I think I want to change my oxygen,
Dm Dm/C♯ Gm C Gm
I think I want to change my air, my atmosphere,
Em A | A ||
I want to reach out.
Solo 1
|: Am | D | Am | D :|
Verse 3
Am F♯m7♭5 C
I wanna be bigger, stronger, drive a faster car
To take me anywhere in seconds,
Dsus2 Am
To take me anywhere I wanna go
F♯m7♭5 C
And drive around my faster car.
I will settle for nothing less,
Dsus2 Am | Am ||
I will settle for nothing less.
Chorus 2
Dm Dm/C♯ Gm
I think I need to change my altitude,
C Gm Em A
I think I want to change my oxygen,
Dm Dm/C♯ Gm C Gm
I think I want to change my air, my atmosphere,
Em A | A ||
I want to reach out.
Solo 2
|: Fmaj7 | G C | D | D :| Play 4 times
|: Am | D | Am | D :|
Verse 4
Am D Am D
Bigger and better, bigger and better,
Am D Am D
Bigger and better, bigger and better,
Am F♯m7♭5 C
Bigger, stronger drive a faster car,
Dsus2 Am
At the touch of a button I can go anywhere I wanna go.

BROTHERS AND SISTERS

Words & Music by
Guy Berryman, Jon Buckland, Will Champion & Chris Martin

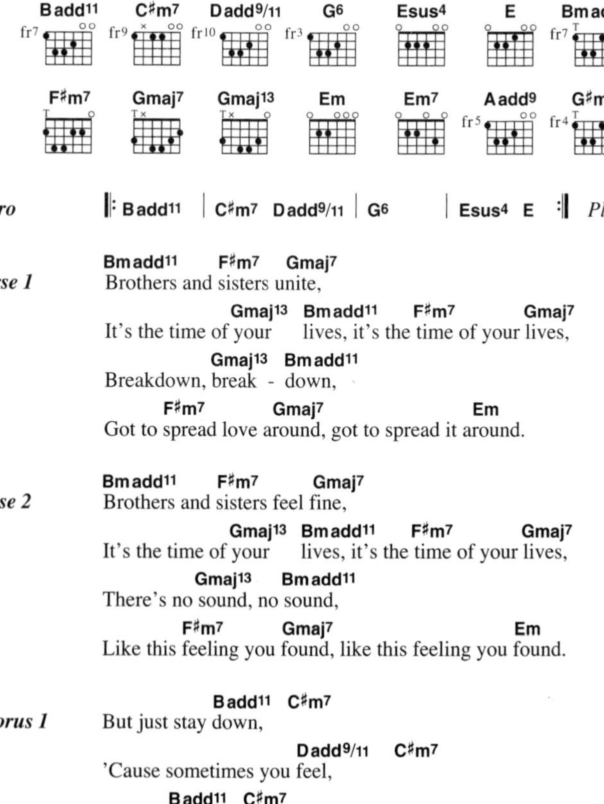

Intro |: Badd11 | C♯m7 Dadd9/11 | G6 | Esus4 E :| *Play 4 times*

Verse 1

```
Bmadd11     F♯m7    Gmaj7
Brothers and sisters unite,
                   Gmaj13   Bmadd11      F♯m7           Gmaj7
It's the time of your       lives, it's the time of your lives,
                 Gmaj13   Bmadd11
Breakdown, break  -  down,
         F♯m7           Gmaj7                      Em
Got to spread love around, got to spread it around.
```

Verse 2

```
Bmadd11     F♯m7         Gmaj7
Brothers and sisters feel fine,
                   Gmaj13   Bmadd11      F♯m7           Gmaj7
It's the time of your       lives, it's the time of your lives,
               Gmaj13     Bmadd11
There's no sound, no sound,
           F♯m7        Gmaj7                          Em
Like this feeling you found, like this feeling you found.
```

Chorus 1

```
                 Badd11  C♯m7
But just stay down,
                               Dadd9/11   C♯m7
'Cause sometimes you feel,
          Badd11  C♯m7
So stay down.
```

cont.

Dadd9/11 C♯m7 Gmaj7
And sometimes you feel,

Em7 Aadd9 Gmaj7
And it's me they're looking for,

Em7 Aadd9 Gmaj7
And it's me, I will never survive,

Em7 Aadd9
But we'll be around some more.

| Gmaj7 | Gmaj13 | Gmaj7 | Gmaj13 ||

Verse 3

Bmadd11 F♯m7 Gmaj7
Brothers and sisters unite,

Gmaj13 Bmadd11 F♯m7 Gmaj7
It's the time of your lives, it's the time of your lives,

Gmaj13 Bmadd11
Breakdown, break - down,

F♯m7 Gmaj7 Em
Got to spread love around, got to spread it all round.

Chorus 2

Badd11 C♯m7
But just stay down,

Dadd9/11 C♯m7
And sometimes you'll feel,

Badd11 C♯m7
So stay around.

Dadd9/11 C♯m7 Gmaj7
And sometimes you'll feel,

Em7 Aadd9 Gmaj7
And it's me they're looking for,

Em7 Aadd9 Gmaj7
And it's me, I will never survive,

Em7 Aadd9
But we'll be around some more.

| Gmaj7 | Gmaj13 | Gmaj7 | Gmaj13 ||

Outro

| Badd11 | C♯m7 Dadd9/11 | G6 | Esus4 E |
It's gonna be al -

| Badd11 | Badd11 G♯m♭6 | F♯m7 | E |
- right. It's gonna be al -

| Badd11 | C♯m7 Dadd9/11 | G6 | F♯m7 |
- right. It's gonna be al -

| Badd11 | C♯m7 Dadd9/11 | G6 | F♯m7 ||
- right.

CAREFUL WHERE YOU STAND

Words & Music by
Guy Berryman, Jon Buckland, Will Champion & Chris Martin

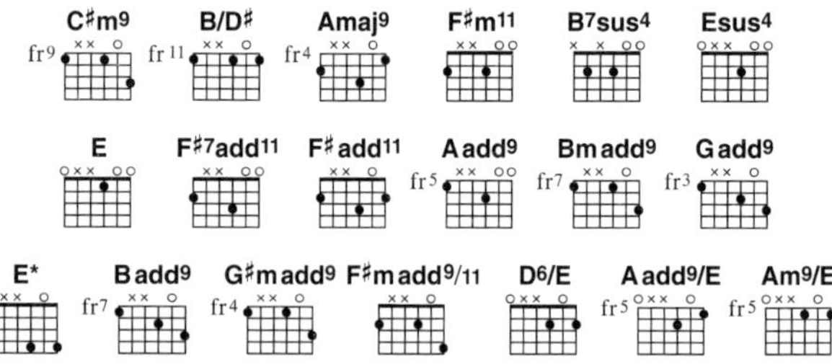

Intro ‖: C♯m9 | C♯m9 B/D♯ | C♯m9 | C♯m9 B/D♯ :‖

Verse 1

```
      C♯m9  B/D♯   C♯m9  B/D♯
I feel safe,  I feel warm
             C♯m9       B/D♯       C♯m9
When you're here, can I do no wrong?
        Amaj9  F♯m11                 C♯m9
I am cured     when I'm by your side,
       B7sus4        Esus4    E
I'm alright, I'm alright.
```

Verse 2

```
        C♯m9       B/D♯    C♯m9
I am safe when I am with you,
       B/D♯    C♯m9       B/D♯          C♯m9
And I feel      warm, if you want me to.
        Amaj9  F♯m11                 C♯m9
I am cured     when I'm by your side,
       F♯7add11   F♯add11
I'm alright.
```

| F♯7add11 F♯add11 | Aadd9 Amaj9 | Aadd9 ‖

Chorus 1

```
Bmadd9              Gadd9     E*     Gadd9
Careful where you stand, my love,
Bmadd9              Gadd9    E*    Gadd9
Careful where you lay your head.
```

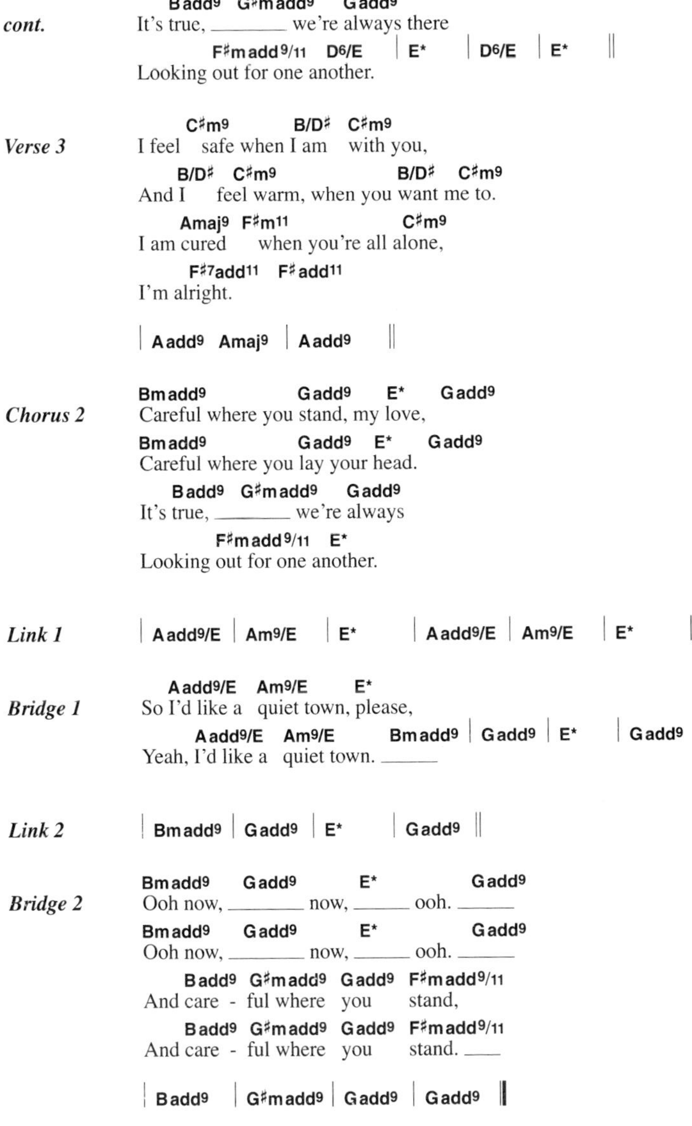

cont.

Badd9 G♯madd9 Gadd9
It's true, ______ we're always there
F♯madd9/11 D6/E | E* | D6/E | E* ||
Looking out for one another.

Verse 3

C♯m9 B/D♯ C♯m9
I feel safe when I am with you,
B/D♯ C♯m9 B/D♯ C♯m9
And I feel warm, when you want me to.
Amaj9 F♯m11 C♯m9
I am cured when you're all alone,
F♯7add11 F♯add11
I'm alright.

| Aadd9 Amaj9 | Aadd9 ||

Chorus 2

Bmadd9 Gadd9 E* Gadd9
Careful where you stand, my love,
Bmadd9 Gadd9 E* Gadd9
Careful where you lay your head.
Badd9 G♯madd9 Gadd9
It's true, ______ we're always
F♯madd9/11 E*
Looking out for one another.

Link 1

| Aadd9/E | Am9/E | E* | Aadd9/E | Am9/E | E* ||

Bridge 1

Aadd9/E Am9/E E*
So I'd like a quiet town, please,
Aadd9/E Am9/E Bmadd9 | Gadd9 | E* | Gadd9 |
Yeah, I'd like a quiet town. ______

Link 2

| Bmadd9 | Gadd9 | E* | Gadd9 ||

Bridge 2

Bmadd9 Gadd9 E* Gadd9
Ooh now, ______ now, ______ ooh. ______
Bmadd9 Gadd9 E* Gadd9
Ooh now, ______ now, ______ ooh. ______
Badd9 G♯madd9 Gadd9 F♯madd9/11
And care - ful where you stand,
Badd9 G♯madd9 Gadd9 F♯madd9/11
And care - ful where you stand. ______

| Badd9 | G♯madd9 | Gadd9 | Gadd9 ||

CLOCKS

Words & Music by
Guy Berryman, Jon Buckland, Will Champion & Chris Martin

D Am Em Amadd11 Em7

Am7 Em/G Fmaj7 C G6 Fmaj9

Capo first fret

Intro ‖: D | Am | Am | Em :‖

‖: D | Am | Am | Em :‖

Verse 1

```
        D                   Amadd11
The lights go out and I can't be saved,
                    Em7
Tides that I tried to swim against
       D                     Amadd11
Have brought me down upon my knees,
             Em7
Oh, I beg, I beg and plead,
          D                  Amadd11
Singing;   come out with things unsaid,
                Em7
Shoot an apple off my head
       D             Amadd11
And a   trouble that can't be named
                    Em7
A tiger's waiting to be tamed singing . . .
```

Chorus 1

```
D     Am       Em
  You ______ are,
D     Am       Em
  You ______ are.
```

Piano Riff 1 ‖: D | Am | Am | Em :‖

Verse 2

D Amadd11
Confusion that never stops,
Em7
The closing walls and ticking clocks
D Amadd11
Gonna come back and take you home
Em7
I could not stop that you now know,
D Amadd11
Singing; come out upon my seas,
Em7
Cursed missed opportunities
D Amadd11
Am I a part of the cure,
Em7
Or am I part of the disease? Singing . . .

Chorus 2

D Am Em
You _____ are,
D Am Em
You _____ are.
D Am Em
You _____ are,
D Am Em
You _____ are.

Instrumental

𝄆 D | Am7 | Am7 | Em/G 𝄇 *x3*

D Am7 Em/G
You _____ are.

Bridge

Fmaj7 C G6
And nothing else compares
Fmaj7 C G6
Oh no nothing else compares,
Fmaj7 C G6 Fmaj7 Fmaj9 Fmaj7 Fmaj
And nothing else compares.

Piano riff 2

𝄆 D | Am | Am | Em 𝄇

𝄆 D | Am7 | Am7 | Em/G 𝄇

Chorus 3

```
D       Am7       Em/G
  You ——— are,
D       Am7       Em/G
  You ——— are.
```

Outro

```
   D         Am7                   Em/G
‖: Home, home, where I wanted to go.
D         Am7                   Em/G
Home, home, where I wanted to go.  :‖
```

Repeat to fade

CRESTS OF WAVES

Words & Music by
Guy Berryman, Jon Buckland, Will Champion & Chris Martin

B7sus4 C♯m F♯m7 G♯m7 B A

Intro | B7sus4 |

| C♯m | F♯m7 G♯m7 | C♯m | F♯m7 G♯m7 |

| C♯m | F♯m7 G♯m7 | F♯m7 | G♯m7 B |

Verse 1

```
                  C♯m                A
It could be worse, I could be alone
                 F♯m7                     G♯m7
I could be locked in here on my own
               C♯m                A
Or like a stone that certainly drops
             F♯m7  G♯m7
It never stops, no.
B                C♯m              A
I could be lost, or I could be saved
             F♯m7                     G♯m7
Calling out from beneath the waves
             C♯m                  A
Beaten down by the sloshing rain
             F♯m7          G♯m7    B
Never again, never again.
```

Chorus 1

```
C♯m      F♯m7      G♯m7
Oo   -   oo    -   oo
C♯m      F♯m7      G♯m7
Oo   -   oo    -   oo
C♯m      F♯m7      G♯m7
Oo   -   oo    -   oo
              F♯m7                    G♯m7
Skating out from the crests of waves.
```

Link 1 | C♯m | F♯m7 G♯m7 | C♯m | F♯m7 G♯m7 |

| C♯m | F♯m7 G♯m7 | F♯m7 | G♯m7 B |

Verse 2

                    C#m   A
It could be worse, it s all sweet
                       F#m7   G#m7
You could be snapped from the jaws of defeat.
             C#m7   A
Or like a light lit up on a beach
                                F#m7   G#m7
Wear your heart on your sleeve, oh.
B   C#m   A
You want to stop before you begin
                 F#m7   G#m7
You want to sink when you know you could swim.
                 C#m   A
You want to stop just before you begin
                 F#m7   G#m7   B
Never give in, never give in.

Chorus 2

C#m   F#m7   G#m7
Oo   -   oo   -   oo
C#m   F#m7   G#m7
Oo   -   oo   -   oo
C#m   F#m7   G#m7
Oo   -   oo   -   oo
            F#m7   G#m7
Skating out from the crests of waves.

Bridge

A
   Nothing matters,
F#m7   G#m7
   Except life and the love we make
A
   Nothing matters
F#m7   G#m7
   Except life and the love we make
A
   Nothing matters
F#m7   G#m7
   Except life and the love we make
F#m7   G#m7
                        Except life and the love we make.

Chorus 3

```
C♯m        F♯m7      G♯m7
Oo    -    oo    -   oo
C♯m        F♯m7      G♯m7
Oo    -    oo    -   oo
C♯m        F♯m7      G♯m7
Oo    -    oo    -   oo
        F♯m7                   G♯m7
Skating out from the crests of waves.
C♯m        F♯m7      G♯m7
Oo    -    oo    -   oo
C♯m        F♯m7      G♯m7
Oo    -    oo    -   oo
C♯m        F♯m7      G♯m7
Oo    -    oo    -   oo
        F♯m7                   G♯m7
Skating out from the crests of waves.
       F♯m7           G♯m7
You re longing to be saved,
           F♯m7                    G♯m7
Screaming out from the crests of waves,
       F♯m7           G♯m7
You re longing to be saved,
           F♯m7                    G♯m7
Screaming out from the crests of waves.
```

DAYLIGHT

Words & Music by
Guy Berryman, Jon Buckland, Will Champion & Chris Martin

F♯5 E6 Gmaj7(♭5) Amaj7 Dmaj7 F♯

Intro ‖: F♯5 | F♯5 | F♯5 | F♯5 :‖

‖: E6 | Gmaj7(♭5) | F♯5 | F♯5 :‖

Verse 1

```
             E6  Gmaj7(♭5)  F♯5
To my sur      -      prise
           E6   Gmaj7(♭5)   F♯5
And my de - light.
          E6  Gmaj7(♭5)    F♯5
I saw sun       -         rise
          E6  Gmaj7(♭5)  F♯5
I saw sun     -      light.
```

Verse 2

```
        E6 Gmaj7(♭5)   F♯5
I am no       -       thing
          E6    Gmaj7(♭5)     F♯5
In the dark.
             E6     Gmaj7(♭5)  F♯5
And the clouds              burst
            E6   Gmaj7(♭5)        F♯5
To show day       -       light.
```

Chorus 1

```
Amaj7                   Dmaj7
Ooh,___ and the sun will shine
F♯                 Amaj7
Yeah,___ on this heart of mine.
                    Dmaj7
Ooh,___ and I realise
F♯                  Amaj7
Who,___ cannot live without
                  Dmaj7          (F♯5)
Ooh,___ come apart without, yeah.
```

Link 1 | F♯5 | F♯5 | F♯5 | F♯5 |

|: E6 | Gmaj7(♭5) | F♯5 | F♯5 :|

Verse 3
E6 Gmaj7(♭5) F♯5
On a hill - top
E6 Gmaj7(♭5) F♯5
On a sky rise.
E6 Gmaj7(♭5) F♯5 E6 Gmaj7(♭5) F♯5
Like a first born child.

Verse 4
E6 Gmaj7(♭5) F♯5
On a full tilt,
E6 Gmaj7(♭5) F♯5
And in full flight
E6 Gmaj7(♭5) F♯5
Defeat dark - ness
E6 Gmaj7(♭5) F♯5
Breaking day - light.

Chorus 2
Amaj7 Dmaj7
Ooh,___ and the sun will shine
F♯ Amaj7
Yeah,___ on this heart of mine.
Dmaj7
Ooh,___ and I realise
F♯ Amaj7
Who,___ cannot live without
Amaj7 Dmaj7 F♯5 | F♯5 | F♯5 | F♯5 ||
Ooh,___ come apart without, daylight.

Outro
E6 Gmaj7(♭5)
|: Slowly breaking through the daylight,
F♯5
Slowly breaking through the daylight. :| *Repeat to fade*

DON'T PANIC

Words & Music by
Guy Berryman, Jon Buckland, Will Champion & Chris Martin

Fmaj7 · Am (fr5) · C · Fmaj9 · Fmaj9♯11 · Dmadd9 (fr10) · Am* · G6 (fr3)

Intro

| Fmaj7 | Fmaj7 | Fmaj7 | Fmaj7 ||

Verse 1

Am — **C** — **Fmaj7** — **Fmaj9**
Bones sinking like stones, all that we've fought for.

Am — **C** — **Fmaj7** — **Fmaj9♯11**
Homes, places we've grown, all of us are done for.

Chorus 1

Dmadd9 — **Am***
But we live in a beautiful world,

G6
Yeah we do, yeah we do,

Dmadd9
We live in a beautiful world | Fmaj7 Fmaj9 | Fmaj7 Fmaj9 ||

Verse 2

As Verse 1

Chorus 2

As Chorus 1

Solo 1

| Am | C | Fmaj7 | Fmaj9 |

| Am | C | Fmaj7 | Fmaj9♯11 ||

Chorus 3

As Chorus 1

Solo 2

As Solo 1

Verse 3

Am — **C** — **Fmaj7** — **Fmaj9**
Oh, all that I know, there's nothing here to run from,

Am — **C** — **Fmaj7**
'Cause yeah, everybody here's got somebody to lean on.

HOW YOU SEE THE WORLD NO. 2

Words & Music by
Guy Berryman, Jon Buckland, Will Champion & Chris Martin

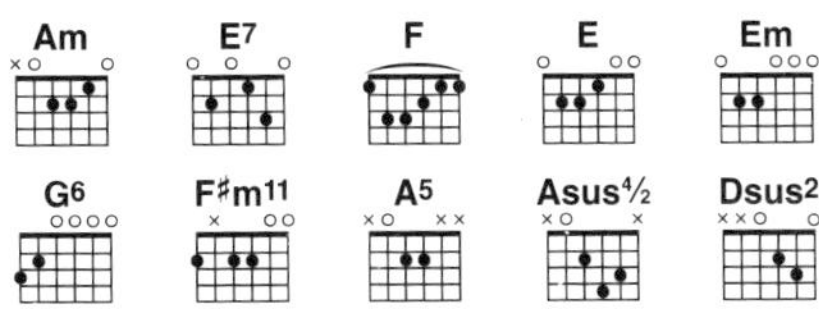

Tune guitar down a semitone

Verse 1

```
                Am
They put the world in a tin can
         E7
Black market contraband.
          Am
And it hurt just a little bit
              E7
When they sliced and packaged it.
      Am
In a long black trench coat
      E7
Two hands around the throat
   F                    Am          E
Oh,   you wanna get it right some - times.
```

Verse 2

```
                Am
There's so much to be scared of
            E7
And not much to make sense of.
                 Am
How did the clowns ever get control?
              E7
But if you hear can you let me know.
            Am
How can they invade it
                 E7
When it's so complicated?
   F                    Am          E
Oh,   you wanna get it right some - times
F                         Am          E
   You just wanna get it right some - times
```

Chorus 1

F Am
It's how you see the world
Em
How many times can you say
F
You can't be - lieve what you heard.
Am
It's how you see the world
G6
Don't you worry yourself
F♯m11
You're not gonna get hurt.
F E
Ooh...

Link 1

𝄆 Am | Am | E7 | E7 𝄇

Verse 3

Am
And there's something missing
E7
Seems like there's nobody listening.
Am
If you're running in a circle
E7
How can you be too careful?
Am
We don't wanna be mantrapped
E7
We don't wanna be shrink wrapped.
F Am E
Oh, just wanna get it right some - times.
F Am E
You just wanna get it right some - times.

```
                F                          Am
Chorus 2           That's how you see the world
                         Em
                How many times have you heard
                        F
                That you can't believe a word?
                                           Am
                   That's how you see the world
                         G6
                Don't you worry yourself
                          F♯m11
                'Cause no - body can hurt.
                F      E7
                You..

                | F   E7  | F   E7  ||


Link 2          |: A5  Asus4/2 | A5         | A5  Asus4/2 | A5       :|


Outro           |: F   Dsus2   | Dsus2      | A5  Asus4/2 | A5       :|


                F       Dsus2          A5       Asus4/2  A5
                   That's how you see the world.
                F       Dsus2          A5       Asus4/2
                   That's how you see the world.
```

EASY TO PLEASE

Words & Music by
Guy Berryman, Jon Buckland, Will Champion & Chris Martin

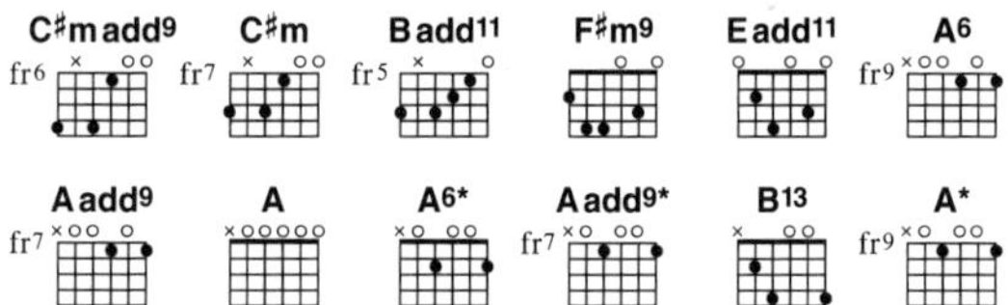

Tune guitar (from bottom string): D, G, D, G, B, D, then Capo second fret

Intro | C♯madd9 | C♯madd9 ||

Verse 1

```
C♯m                    Badd11
Love, I hope we get old,
                   F♯m9                 Eadd11
I hope we can find a way of seeing it all.
  C♯m                  Badd11
Love, I hope we can be,
               F♯m9
I hope I can find a way
                   A6  Aadd9  A6  Aadd9
Of letting you see
      A   A6*  Aadd9*  A6*   A
That I'm so   ea  -  -  sy  to please,
A6*  Aadd9*  A6*
So   ea  -  -  -  (sy.)

| B13  Aadd9*  A*  | B13  Aadd9*  A*  |
  -  -  sy.

| B13  Aadd9*  A*  | B13  Aadd9*  A*  ||
```

Verse 2

```
   C♯m                    Badd11
Love, I hope we grow old,
                  F♯m9                     Eadd11
I hope we can find a way of seeing it all.
   C♯m                  Badd11
Love, I hope we can be,
               F♯m9
I hope I can find a way
                  A6  Aadd9  A6  Aadd9
Of letting you see
      A    A6*  Aadd9*  A6*   A
That I'm so   ea  -  -  sy  to please,
A6*  Aadd9*  A6*
So   ea  -  -  -  (sy.)

| B13  Aadd9*  A* | B13  Aadd9*  A* |
  -  -  sy.

| B13  Aadd9*  A* | B13  Aadd9*  A* ||
```

EVERYTHING'S NOT LOST

Words & Music by
Guy Berryman, Jon Buckland, Will Champion & Chris Martin

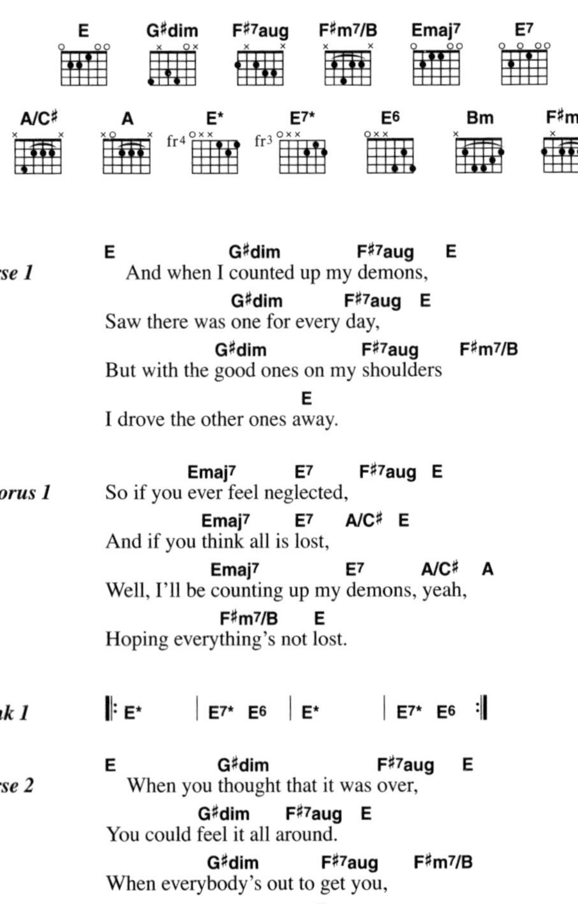

Verse 1

E G♯dim F♯7aug E
And when I counted up my demons,
G♯dim F♯7aug E
Saw there was one for every day,
G♯dim F♯7aug F♯m7/B
But with the good ones on my shoulders
E
I drove the other ones away.

Chorus 1

Emaj7 E7 F♯7aug E
So if you ever feel neglected,
Emaj7 E7 A/C♯ E
And if you think all is lost,
Emaj7 E7 A/C♯ A
Well, I'll be counting up my demons, yeah,
F♯m7/B E
Hoping everything's not lost.

Link 1

𝄆 E* | E7* E6 | E* | E7* E6 𝄇

Verse 2

E G♯dim F♯7aug E
When you thought that it was over,
G♯dim F♯7aug E
You could feel it all around.
G♯dim F♯7aug F♯m7/B
When everybody's out to get you,
E
Don't you let it drag you down.

Chorus 2 As Chorus 1

Link 2 𝄆 E* | E7* E6 | E* | E7* E6 𝄇

Chorus 3 As Chorus 1

Outro

```
                  E*                    E7*  E6
Singing out ah, ah ah yeah,   ah ah yeah,
E*                E7*   E6                  E*
Ah ah yeah,   and everything's not lost,
                        E7*  E6          E*
So come on, yeah,   ah ah yeah,
                     E7*    E6                    E*
Come on, yeah,   and everything's not lost.

                  E7*  E6            E*
Ah ah yeah,   ah ah yeah,
                  E7*   E6                  E*
Ah ah yeah,   and everything's not lost,
                     E7*  E6          E*
Come on yeah,   ah ah yeah,
                        E7*  E6
A-come on yeah.

E                          Bm                  F♯m9
   A-come on yeah,   ah ah yeah,
                                              E
Come on yeah, and everything's not lost.
                    Bm             F♯m9
Sing out yeah,   ah ah yeah,
                                              E
Come on yeah, and everything's not lost.
                     Bm            F♯m9
Come on yeah,   ah ah yeah,
                                             E      Bm    F♯m
Sing out yeah, and everything's not lost.
```

FIX YOU

Words & Music by
Guy Berryman, Jon Buckland, Will Champion & Chris Martin

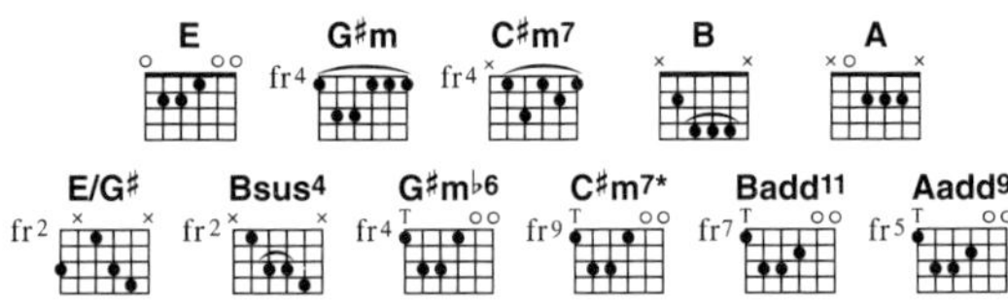

Intro | E G♯m | C♯m7 B | E G♯m | C♯m7 B ||

Verse 1

```
                 E                     G♯m              C♯m7  B
When you try your best but you don't  succeed,______
                 E                       G♯m                  C♯m7  B
When you get what you want but not what you need,______
                 E                  G♯m              C♯m7  B
When you feel so tired but you can't sleep,______
                   E       G♯m   C♯m7  B
Stuck in re - verse.____________
              E                     G♯m             C♯m7  B
And the tears come streaming down your face______
                 E                    G♯m           C♯m7  B
When you lose something you can't replace,______
              E                     G♯m          C♯m7  B
When you love someone but it goes to waste...______
                  E       G♯m   C♯m7  B
Could it be worse?____________
```

Chorus 1

```
A         E/G♯    Bsus4   B      A
  Lights will__ guide__ you home
      E/G♯  Bsus4  B        A
And ig  -  nite____ your bones,
    E/G♯    Bsus4  B
I__ will__ try_____ to fix you.
```

Instrumental 1 | E G♯m | C♯m7 B | E G♯m | C♯m7 B ||

Verse 2

E G♯m♭6 C♯m7* Badd11
High up above and down below,______

E G♯m♭6 C♯m7* Badd11
When you're too in love to let it go,______

E G♯m♭6 C♯m7* Badd11
But if you never try you'll never know ______

E G♯m♭6 C♯m7* Badd11
Just what you're worth.______

Chorus 2

A E/G♯ Bsus4 B A
Lights will__ guide__ you home

E/G♯ Bsus4 B A
And ig - nite___ your bones,

E/G♯ Bsus4 B
I__ will__ try___ to fix you.

Instrumental 2 |: E | Aadd9 | E | Badd11 |

| C♯m7* | Aadd9 | E | Badd11 :|

Bridge

E Aadd9
Tears stream down your face

E Badd11
When you lose something you cannot replace,

C♯m7* Aadd9 E Badd11
Tears stream down your face and I...___

E Aadd9
Tears stream down your face,

E Badd11
I promise you I will learn from my mistakes.

C♯m7* Aadd9 E Badd11
Tears stream down your face and I...___

Outro

A E/G♯ Bsus4 B A
Lights will__ guide__ you home

E/G♯ Bsus4 B A
And ig - nite___ your bones,

E/G♯ Bsus4 B E
And I__ will__ try___ to fix you.__

FOR YOU

Words & Music by
Guy Berryman, Jon Buckland, Will Champion & Chris Martin

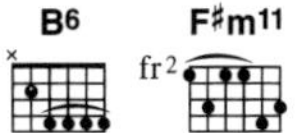

Intro | B6 | B6 |

|: B6 | F♯m11 | B6 | F♯m11 :|

Verse 1

B6 F♯m11
If you're lost and feel alone,
B6 F♯m11
Circumnavigate the globe,
B6 F♯m11
All you ever have to hope for too.
B6 F♯m11
And the way you seem to flow,
B6 F♯m11
Circumnavigate and hope,
B6 F♯m11 B6 F♯m11
And I seem to lose control, with you.

Chorus 1

B6 F♯m11
Ah, ________
B6 F♯m11
Ah, ________
B6 F♯m11
Ah, ________
B6 F♯m11
Ah. ________

Link 1 |: B6 | F♯m11 | B6 | F♯m11 :|

Verse 2

```
B6                         F#m11
   Every one of us is hurt,
B6                              F#m11
   And every one of us is scarred,
B6                         F#m11          B6     F#m11
   Every one of us is scared but not you.
      B6           F#m11
And when your eyes close,
B6       F#m11
   Your head hurts,
B6       F#m11    B6       F#m11
   Your eyes like stone.
```

Chorus 2

```
B6         F#m11
Ah, ______
B6         F#m11
Ah, ______
B6         F#m11
Ah, ______
B6         F#m11
Ah. ______
```

Link 2

```
| B6     | F#m11  | B6     | F#m11  ||
```

Verse 3

```
B6                         F#m11
   Every one of us is scared,
B6                         F#m11
   Every one of us is hurt,
B6                    F#m11    B6     F#m11
   Every one has hope for you.
```

Outro

```
       B6    F#m11
||: For you,          :||   Play 6 times
    B6    F#m11
For you.

| B6       | F#m11     |
    B6    F#m11
For you.
    B6    F#m11
For you.

| B6       | F#m11     | B6        ||
```

GOD PUT A SMILE UPON YOUR FACE

Words & Music by
Guy Berryman, Jon Buckland, Will Champion & Chris Martin

D♭ E6 E♭7 Dmaj7 Amaj7 F♯add9

fr3 fr8 fr5

Tune down three semitones

Intro | D♭ | E6 | E♭7 | E♭7 Dmaj7 |
| D♭ | E6 | E♭7 | Dmaj7 ||

Verse 1
```
D♭                E6               E♭7    Dmaj7
   Where do we go, nobody knows?
D♭           E6           E♭7         Dmaj7
   I've gotta say I'm on my way ___ down.
D♭               E6                     E♭7     Dmaj7
   God give me style and give me grace.
D♭             E6              E♭7        Dmaj7
   God put a smile upon my face. ________
```

Guitar Solo 1 | D♭ | E6 | E♭7 | E♭7 Dmaj7 |
| D♭ | E6 | E♭7 | Dmaj7 ||

Verse 2
```
D♭                E6                  E♭7    Dmaj7
   Where do we go to draw the line?
D♭            E6                 E♭7          Dmaj7
   I've gotta say I've wasted all your time, honey, honey
D♭              E6               E♭7          Dmaj7
   Where do I go to fall from grace?
D♭             E6                E♭7     Dmaj7
   God put a smile upon your face. Yeah.
```

Chorus 1
```
      Amaj7                          E6            F♯add9                Amaj7
And ah ____   when you work it out I'm worse than you. _____
                                  E6          F♯add9      Amaj7
Yeah, _____  when you work it out I wanted to. _____
                                 E6                  F♯add9            Amaj7
And ah _____  when you work out where to draw the line, _____
                       E6     F♯add9
Your guess is as good as mine.
```

Guitar Solo 2 | D♭ | E6 | E♭7 | E♭7 Dmaj7 |

| D♭ | E6 | E♭7 | Dmaj7 ||

Verse 3

D♭ E6 E♭7 Dmaj7
Where do we go, nobody knows?
D♭ E6 E♭7 Dmaj7
Don't ever say you're on your way down.
D♭ E6 E♭7 Dmaj7
When God gave you style and gave you grace,
D♭ E6 E♭7 Dmaj7
And put a smile upon your face, ah yeah.

Chorus 2

Amaj7 E6 F♯add9 Amaj7
And ah, when you work it out I'm worse than you. ____
E6 F♯add9 Amaj7
Yeah, when you work it out I wanted to. ____
E6 F♯add9 Amaj7
And ah, when you work out where to draw the line, ____
E6 F♯add9 D♭ E6 E♭7
Your guess is as good as mine. ____
Dmaj7 D♭ E6 E♭7
It's as good as mine. ____
Dmaj7 D♭ E6 E♭7
It's as good as mine. ____
Dmaj7 D♭ E6
It's as good as mine. ____
E♭7
Na na na na na na na na na na
Dmaj7 Amaj7 E6
It's as good as mine. ____
F♯add9 Amaj7 E6
It's as good as mine. ____
F♯add9 Amaj7 E6 F♯add9
It's as good as mine. ____

Outro

D♭ E6 E♭7 Dmaj7
Where do we go, nobody knows?
D♭ E6 E♭7 Dmaj7
Don't ever say you're on your way down.
D♭ E6 E♭7 Dmaj7
When God gave you style and gave you grace,
D♭ E6 E♭7 Dmaj7
And put a smile upon your face.

GRAVITY

Words & Music by
Guy Berryman, Jon Buckland, Will Champion & Chris Martin

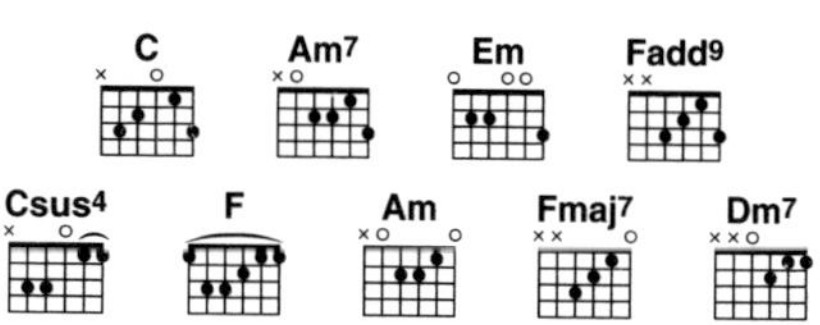

Capo third fret

Intro ||: C | Am7 | Em | Fadd9 :||

Verse 1

```
C                  Am7            Em
Baby, it's been a long time com - ing
         Fadd9     C
Such a long, long time.
       Am7          Em
And I can't stop run - ning
         Fadd9     C
Such a long, long time.
           Am7          Em
Can you hear my heart beating?
           Fadd9    C
Can you hear that sound?
       Am7      Em
'Cos I can't help thinking
      F          C     Csus4  C
And I won't stop now.
```

Chorus 1

```
          F
And then I looked up at the sun
              C
And I could see
        Am                            Fmaj7
Oh, the way that gravity pulls on you and me.

And then I looked up at the sky
               C
And saw the sun
```

cont.

```
           Am                                   Fmaj7
And the way that gravity pushes on every - one.
             Dm7
On every - one.
```

Verse 2

```
C                  Am7        Em
Baby, when your wheels stop turning
           Fadd9  C
And you feel let down.
        Am7       Em
And it seems like troubles
              Fadd9    C
Have come all___ a - round.
      Am7            Em
I can hear your heart beating
      Fadd9   C
I can hear that sound.
      Am7      Em
But I can't help thinking
        Fadd9      C     Csus4   C
And I won't look now.
```

Chorus 2

```
          F
And then I looked up at the sun
             C
And I could see
        Am                                Fmaj7
Oh, the way that gravity pulls on you and me.

And then I looked up at the sky
             C
And saw the sun
           Am                                   Fmaj7
And the way that gravity pushes on every - one.
             Dm7
On every - one.

On everyone.
```

Outro

```
||: C     | Am7    | Em     | Fadd9  :||  Play 4 times

| C     ||
```

GREEN EYES

Words & Music by
Guy Berryman, Jon Buckland, Will Champion & Chris Martin

A E/G♯ Bmadd11 Dsus2 F♯m7 G6 Dadd9/F♯ Bm

Verse 1

A E/G♯ Bmadd11
Honey you are a rock,
A E/G♯ Bmadd11
Upon which I stand.
A E/G♯ Bmadd11
And I come here to talk,
A E/G♯ Bmadd11
I hope you understand.

Verse 2

Bmadd11
That Green Eyes,
Dsus2
Yeah the spot light
A E/G♯
Shines upon you.
Bmadd11 Dsus2
And how could anybody,
A E/G♯ F♯m7
Deny you?

Chorus 1

Bmadd11 Dsus2
I came here with a load,
A G6 Dadd9/F♯
And it feels so much light - er now I met you.
Bmadd11 Dsus2
And honey you should know,
A G6 Dsus2
That I could never go on without you.
Bmadd11 | Bmadd11 | Bmadd11 | Bmadd11 ||
Green Eyes.

Verse 3

A   E/G#   Bmadd11
Honey you   are the sea,
A   E/G#   Bmadd11
Upon which I float.
A   E/G#   Bmadd11
And I came here to talk,
A   E/G#   Bmadd11
I think you should know.

Verse 4

Bmadd11
That Green Eyes,
Dsus2   A   E/G#
You're the one that I wanted to find.
Bmadd11
And any-one who
Dsus2
Tried to deny you
A   E/G# F#m7
Must be out of their minds.

Chorus 2

Bmadd11   Dsus2
Because I came here with a load,
A G6   Dadd9/F#
And it feels so much light - er since I met you.
Bmadd11   Dsus2
And honey you should know,
A   G6   Dsus2
That I could never go on   without you.
Bm
Green Eyes,

Green Eyes,
A
Oh oh oh.
Bm
Oh oh oh.

Oh oh oh.

Outro

A   E/G#   Bmadd11
Honey you   are a rock
A   E/G#   Bmadd11
Upon which I stand.

THE HARDEST PART

Words & Music by
Guy Berryman, Jon Buckland, Will Champion & Chris Martin

C Em A7sus4 Dsus4 D Em7
G Bm11 G6 Em/D G6/B Cadd9

Capo third fret

Intro | C | Em | A7sus4 | A7sus4 |
| C | C | Dsus4 D | D ||

Verse 1
```
Em7       C
  And the hardest part
     G                 Bm11
Was letting go not taking part,
Em7        C              G  Bm11
  Was the hardest part,________
Em7       C
  And the strangest thing
     G6                Bm11
Was waiting for that bell to ring,
G6            C              G   Bm11
  It was the strangest start.________
```

Chorus 1
```
C                  G      D
  I could feel it go down,___
C                     G          D
  Bittersweet I could taste in my mouth,
C                    G      D
  Silver lining, the clouds,
             Em  Em/D  C  G6/B  Am
Oh, and I,___________________________

I wish that I could work it out.
```

Instrumental 1 ||: Em7 | Cadd9 | G | Bm11 :||

Verse 2

```
Em7          C
  And the hardest part
      G               Bm11
Was letting go not taking part,
Em7           C          G     Bm11
  You really broke my heart.___
Em7       C
  And I tried to sing
      G6                   Bm11
But I couldn't think of anything,
G6            C            G    Bm11
  It was the hardest part.____
```

Chorus 2

```
C                      G      D
  I could feel it go down,__
C                           G              D
  You left the sweetest taste in my mouth,
C                      G       D
  Silver lining, the clouds,
              Em   Em/D  C  G6/B  Am
Oh, and I,____________________________
              Em   Em/D  C  G6/B  D
Oh, and I,____________________________

I wonder what it's all about.
```

Instrumental 2

```
|: C        | Em       | A7sus4   | A7sus4   :| Play 3 times

 | C        | C        | D        | D        ||
```

Bridge

```
                   C     Em    A7sus4
Everything I know is__ wrong,
                  C          Em          A7sus4
Everything I do it just comes un - done,
                   C    Em   A7sus4
Everything is torn apart,______
                         C
Oh, and that's the hardest part.
                Dsus4       D
That's the hardest part,__
                       C
Yeah, that's the hardest part,
                Dsus4      D
That's the hardest part.
```

Outro

```
|: C        | Em       | A7sus4   | A7sus4   :| Play 4 times to fade
```

HELP IS ROUND THE CORNER

Words & Music by
Guy Berryman, Jon Buckland, Will Champion & Chris Martin

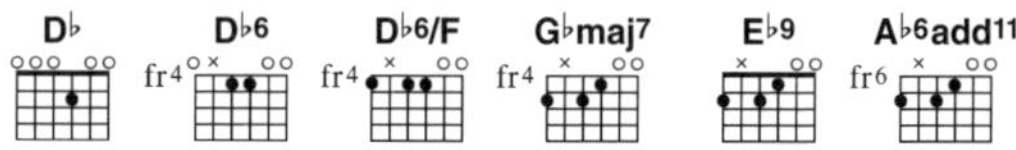

Tune guitar (from bottom string): D♭, A♭, D♭, G♭, D♭, F

Intro | D♭ | D♭6 | D♭ | D♭6 ||

Verse 1

```
D♭                                D♭6
Stuck here in the middle of nowhere
         D♭                          D♭6
With a headache, and a heavy heart.
       D♭                          D♭6
Well, nothing was going quite right here,
           D♭                       D♭6    D♭6/F
And I'm tired, I can't play my part.
```

Chorus 1

```
G♭maj7
   Oh, come on, come on,
             E♭9
Oh what a state I'm in,
G♭maj7
   Oh, come on, come on,
                E♭9
Why won't it just sink in
      D♭                          A♭6add11        D♭   A♭6add11
That help is just around the corner for us?
```

Verse 2

```
     D♭                             D♭6
Oh, my head just won't stop aching,
           D♭                      D♭6
And I'm sat here licking my wounds
           D♭                                   D♭6
And I'm shattered, but it really doesn't matter
              D♭                            D♭6      D♭6/F
'Cause my rescue is gonna be here soon.
```

```
            G♭maj7
Chorus 2       Oh, come on, come on,
                         E♭9
            Oh what a state I'm in,
            G♭maj7
               Oh, come on, come on,
                           E♭9
            Why won't it just sink in
                D♭                     A♭6add11    D♭    A♭6add11
            That help is just around the corner for us? ___
                D♭                     A♭6add11    D♭    E♭9
            That help is just around the corner for us. ___
                   G♭maj7                   A♭6add11    D♭
            Oh, that help is just around the corner for us. ___
```

HIGH SPEED

Words & Music by
Guy Berryman, Jon Buckland, Will Champion & Chris Martin

B♭6/9 | Csus2/4 fr3 | Gadd9 fr6 | E♭maj7♯11 fr7 | E♭maj7 fr8 | E♭maj9 fr6 | B♭6 fr3 | Cadd9 fr5

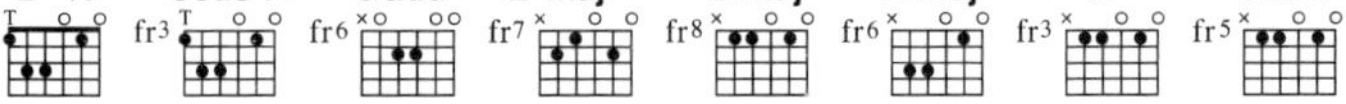

Tune guitar (from bottom string): D, G, D, G, B, D

Intro

|: B♭6/9 | Csus2/4 | B♭6/9 | Csus2/4 :|

| Gadd9 | Gadd9 | Gadd9 | Gadd9 ||

Verse 1

E♭maj7♯11 Gadd9 E♭maj7♯11
Can anybody fly this thing?

Before my head explodes,
E♭maj7 E♭maj9 Gadd9
Before my head starts to ring.
E♭maj7 E♭maj9 Gadd9 B♭6
We've been living life inside a bubble,
Cadd9 Gadd9
We've been living life inside a bubble.

Chorus 1

B♭6/9 Csus2/4
And confidence in you
B♭6/9
Is confidence in me,
Csus2/4 Gadd9
Is confidence in high speed.

Verse 2

E♭maj7♯11 Gadd9 E♭maj7♯11
Can anybody stop this thing?

Before my head explodes,
E♭maj7 E♭maj9 Gadd9
Before my head starts to ring.
E♭maj7 E♭maj9 Gadd9 B♭6
We've been living life inside a bubble,
Cadd9 Gadd9
We've been living life inside a bubble.

Chorus 2

```
B♭6/9                      Csus2/4
   And confidence in you
                  B♭6/9
Is confidence in me,
                  Csus2/4  Gadd9
Is confidence in high      speed,

In high speed, high speed.
```

Link

```
| Gadd9  | Gadd9  | Gadd9  | Gadd9  ||
```

Outro

```
B♭6/9             Csus2/4         B♭6/9
   And high speed you want,
          Csus2/4        B♭6/9
High speed you want,
          Csus2/4        B♭6/9   Csus2/4
High speed you want,
                         Gadd9
High speed you want.

|: Gadd9  | Gadd9  :|  Repeat to fade
```

I BLOOM BLAUM

Words & Music by
Guy Berryman, Jon Buckland, Will Champion & Chris Martin

D(♯11) Dadd9 D Gm(add11)

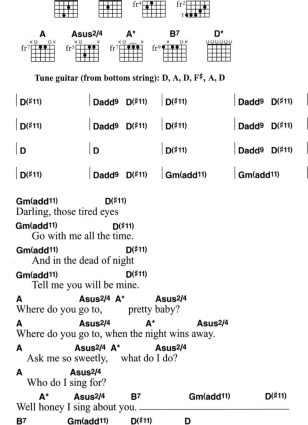

A Asus2/4 A* B7 D*

Tune guitar (from bottom string): D, A, D, F♯, A, D

Intro

D(♯11)	Dadd9 D(♯11)	D(♯11)	Dadd9 D(♯11)
D(♯11)	Dadd9 D(♯11)	D(♯11)	Dadd9 D(♯11)
D	D	D(♯11)	Dadd9 D(♯11)
D(♯11)	Dadd9 D(♯11)	Gm(add11)	Gm(add11)

Verse

```
Gm(add11)               D(♯11)
Darling, those tired eyes
Gm(add11)                  D(♯11)
   Go with me all the time.
Gm(add11)                      D(♯11)
   And in the dead of night
Gm(add11)                      D(♯11)
   Tell me you will be mine.
A                Asus2/4  A*         Asus2/4
Where do you go to,         pretty baby?
A                Asus2/4          A*          Asus2/4
Where do you go to, when the night wins away.
A              Asus2/4  A*          Asus2/4
  Ask me so sweetly,      what do I do?
A            Asus2/4
  Who do I sing for?
     A*        Asus2/4       B7            Gm(add11)          D(♯11)
Well honey I sing about you. ______________________________
B7           Gm(add11)     D(♯11)       D
You. ________________________________
```

I RAN AWAY

Words & Music by
Guy Berryman, Jon Buckland, Will Champion & Chris Martin

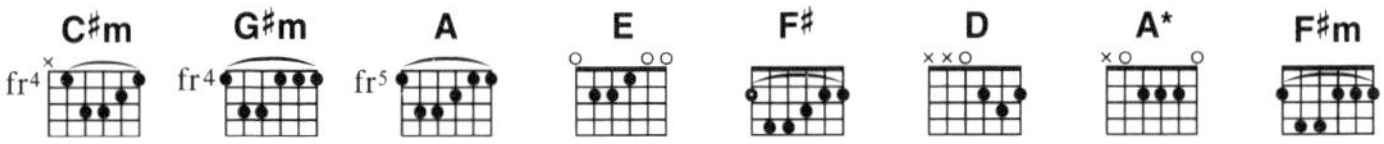

C♯m fr4 | G♯m fr4 | A fr5 | E | F♯ | D | A* | F♯m

Intro

```
N.C.
One, two, three . . . well

| N.C.       | N.C.       | N.C.       | N.C.       ||

||: C♯m   G♯m | A     G♯m | C♯m   G♯m | A     G♯m :||
```

Verse 1

```
C♯m         G♯m
   I ran away from you
A                G♯m
   That's all I ever do
C♯m                   G♯m
   And though I started here
A            G♯m
   I ran away from you.
C♯m                  G♯m
   I'm gonna come on in
A            G♯m
   And see it through.

| C♯m   G♯m | A     G♯m |
```

Verse 2

```
C♯m         G♯m
   I ran away from you
A                    G♯m
   That's all I ever do
C♯m                      G♯m
   And when I heard you call
A                     G♯m
   To come back to you.
C♯m                        G♯m
   And though I should stay
A                               G♯m
   I don't have the stomach to.

| C♯m   G♯m | A     G♯m |
```

Chorus 1

E   F♯
  Everyone I know,
                D   A*
Says I'm a fool to mess with you,
E   F♯
  Everyone I know
               D   A*
Says it's a stupid thing to do.
E   F♯
  I have your love on call
                 D   A*
And yet my day was so full
                     D   A*
There might be nothing left to do
      D   A*
So I ran away from you.

Link

‖: C♯m G♯m | A G♯m | C♯m G♯m | A G♯m :‖

Verse 3

C♯m   G♯m
  I'm gonna come on in
A   G♯m
  My eyes are closed.
C♯m   G♯m
  I can feel it there
A   G♯m
  The sun's so close.
C♯m   G♯m
  I'm gonna come on out
A   G♯m
  And burn the sky.

| C♯m G♯m | A G♯m |

Verse 4

C♯m   G♯m
  A star arose,
A   G♯m
  In my own cage
C♯m   G♯m
  I'm stuck in line
A   G♯m
  And in a cage
C♯m   G♯m
  Just a single star
A   G♯m
  I see it fall.

cont. | C♯m G♯m | A G♯m |

Chorus 2

```
E         F♯
   Everyone I know,
              D                    A*
Says I'm a fool to mess with you,
E         F♯
   Everyone I know
             D                A*
Says it's a stupid thing to do.
E                F♯
   I have your love on call
               D          A*
And yet my day was so full
                   D               A*
There might be nothing left to do
     D              A*
So I ran away from you.
```

Outro

```
                           x7
|: C♯m      | F♯m     :| C♯m      | A        |
                                             x3
|: E        | F♯       | D        | A       :|

| D         | A        | D        | A        ||
```

IN MY PLACE

Words & Music by
Guy Berryman, Jon Buckland, Will Champion & Chris Martin

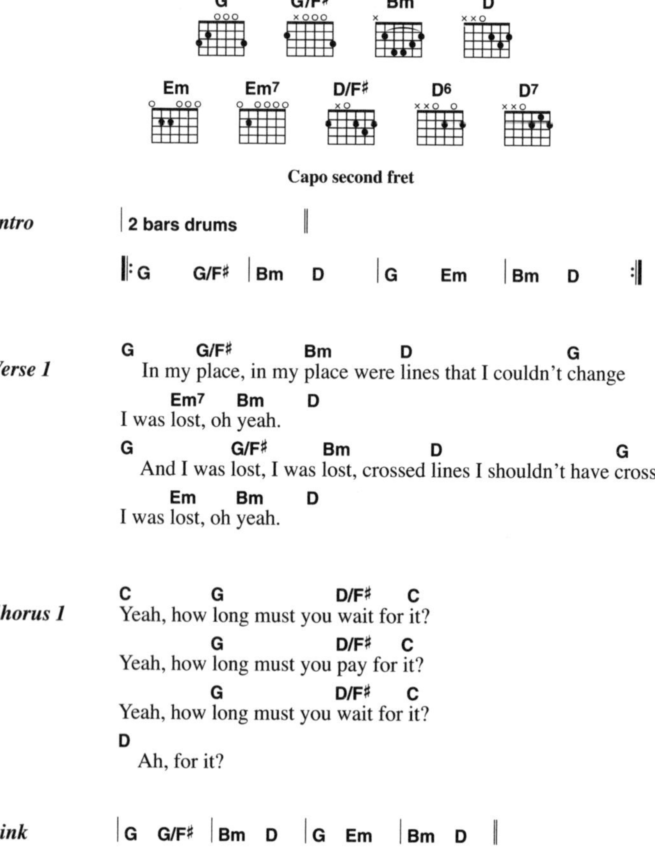

Capo second fret

Intro | 2 bars drums ||

|: G G/F♯ | Bm D | G Em | Bm D :|

Verse 1

```
G          G/F♯            Bm           D                   G
    In my place, in my place were lines that I couldn't change
          Em7     Bm       D
I was lost, oh yeah.
G                G/F♯          Bm              D                       G
    And I was lost, I was lost, crossed lines I shouldn't have crossed
          Em      Bm       D
I was lost, oh yeah.
```

Chorus 1

```
C               G                   D/F♯     C
Yeah, how long must you wait for it?
                G                   D/F♯     C
Yeah, how long must you pay for it?
                G                   D/F♯     C
Yeah, how long must you wait for it?
D
    Ah, for it?
```

Link | G G/F♯ | Bm D | G Em | Bm D ||

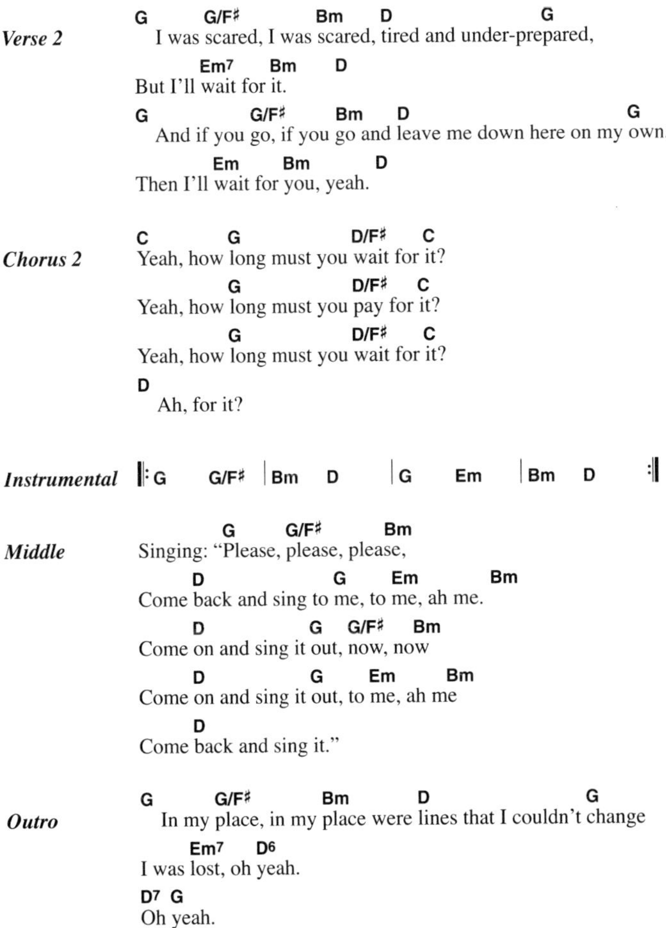

Verse 2

G G/F♯ Bm D G
I was scared, I was scared, tired and under-prepared,
Em7 Bm D
But I'll wait for it.
G G/F♯ Bm D G
And if you go, if you go and leave me down here on my own,
Em Bm D
Then I'll wait for you, yeah.

Chorus 2

C G D/F♯ C
Yeah, how long must you wait for it?
G D/F♯ C
Yeah, how long must you pay for it?
G D/F♯ C
Yeah, how long must you wait for it?
D
Ah, for it?

Instrumental

𝄆 G G/F♯ | Bm D | G Em | Bm D 𝄇

Middle

G G/F♯ Bm
Singing: "Please, please, please,
D G Em Bm
Come back and sing to me, to me, ah me.
D G G/F♯ Bm
Come on and sing it out, now, now
D G Em Bm
Come on and sing it out, to me, ah me
D
Come back and sing it."

Outro

G G/F♯ Bm D G
In my place, in my place were lines that I couldn't change
Em7 D6
I was lost, oh yeah.
D7 G
Oh yeah.

LIFE IS FOR LIVING

Words & Music by
Guy Berryman, Jon Buckland, Will Champion & Chris Martin

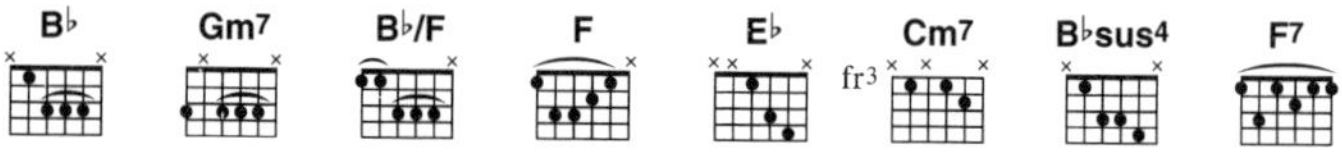

B♭ Gm7 B♭/F F E♭ Cm7 B♭sus4 F7

Tune guitar (from bottom string): E, A, D, G, B, D

Verse 1

B♭ Gm7 B♭/F F
Now I never meant to do you wrong,
E♭ Cm7 B♭ B♭sus4 B♭
That's what I came here to say.
Gm7 B♭/F F
But if I was wrong then I'm sorry,
E♭ Cm7 B♭ B♭sus4 B♭
Then I don't let it stand in our way.

Verse 2

Gm7 B♭/F F
'Cause my head just aches when I think of
E♭ Cm7 B♭ B♭sus4 B♭
The things that I shouldn't have done,
Gm7 B♭/F F
But life is for living, we all know,
E♭ Cm7 B♭ B♭sus4 B♭
And I don't want to live it alone.

Bridge

F F7
Sing ah ah ah,
E♭
Sing ah ah ah,
F F7
And you sing ah ah ah.

Coda

B♭	Gm7	B♭/F	F
E♭	Cm7	B♭ B♭sus4	B♭
B♭	Gm7	B♭/F	F
E♭	Cm7	B♭ B♭sus4	B♭ ‖

LOW

Words & Music by
Guy Berryman, Jon Buckland, Will Champion & Chris Martin

C A7sus4 Em7 A7
Em D Bm G A7/G

Intro
C	C	A7sus4	A7sus4
Em7	Em7	A7	A7
C	C	C	C	

Verse 1
```
Em                          D          Bm
  You see the world in black and white,
    C           A7sus4  Em
No colour or light,
                               D      Bm
You think you'll never get it right;
                 C                A7sus4  Em
But you're wrong, you might.
                                  D        Bm
The sky could fall, could fall on you,
       C           A7sus4      Em
The parting of the sea,——
                                    D           Bm
But you mean more, mean more to me
                C                 A7sus4
Than any colour I can see.
```

Instrumental 1 | Em | Em | Em | Em ||

```
               C                                A7sus4
Chorus 1         All you ever wanted was love
                                              Em7
               But you never look hard enough,
                                                A7
               It's never gonna give itself up.
               C                              A7sus4
                 All you ever wanted to be,
                                                 Em7
               Living in perfect symme - try,
                                                    A7    (C)
               But nothing is as down or as up as us.
```

```
Instrumental 2 | C       | C       | C       | C       |
               (us.)
               | Em      | Em   D  | Bm      | Bm      |

               | C       | A7sus4  | Em      | Em      ||
```

```
               Em                          D        Bm
Verse 2          You see the world in black and white,
                   C       A7sus4  Em
               Not painted right.
                                         D       Bm
               You see no meaning to your life,
                              C   A7sus4   Em
               You should try,____________
                              C   A7sus4   (Em)
               You should try.____________
```

```
Instrumental 3 | Em      | Em      | Em      | Em      ||
```

Chorus 2

C A7sus4
All you ever wanted was love
Em7
But you never look hard e - nough,
A7
It's never gonna give itself up.
C A7sus4
All you ever wanted to be,
Em7
Living in perfect symme - try
A7
But nothing is as down or as up,
C A7sus4
Don't you want to see it come soon?
Em7
Floating in a big white bal - loon,
A7
Or flying on your own silver spoon.
C A7sus4
Don't you want to see it come down,
Em7
There for throwing your arms a - round
A7
Saying, "Not a moment too soon."

Bridge

G A7/G
'Cos I feel low,
G A7/G
'Cos I feel low, oh...
G C A7/G
But I feel low, oh no.

Instrumental 4

| G | A7/G | G | A7/G |
| G | Em7 | A7sus4 | A7sus4 ‖

Outro

G A7/G
Oh, 'cos I feel low,
G A7/G
'Cos I feel low, oh,
G C A7sus4
But I feel low, oh no,
G
Oh.___

A MESSAGE

Words & Music by
Guy Berryman, Jon Buckland, Will Champion & Chris Martin

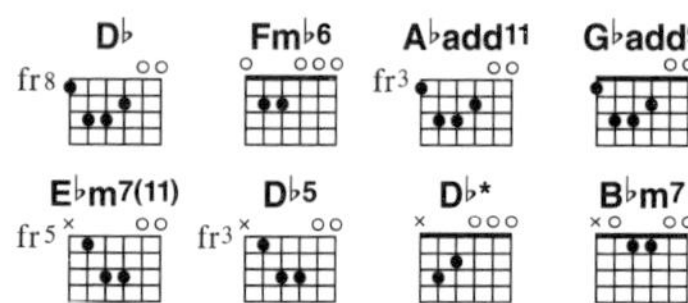

Tune guitar (from bottom string): F, B♭, E♭, A♭, A♭, D♭

Verse 1

```
D♭               Fm♭6  A♭add11
My song is love,
D♭               Fm♭6     A♭add11
Love to the loveless shown
D♭               Fm♭6  A♭add11
And it goes up.

              G♭add9      Fm♭6       A♭add11
You don't have___ to be___ a - lone.
```

Verse 2

```
D♭               Fm♭6  A♭add11
Your heavy heart
D♭             Fm♭6  A♭add11  G♭add9
Is made of stone
D♭             Fm♭6    A♭add11
And it's so hard to see clearly.

              G♭add9     Fm♭6     A♭add11
You don't have to be on your own,
              G♭add9     Fm♭6     A♭add11
You don't have to be on your own.
```

Chorus 1

```
E♭m7(11)                       D♭5    A♭add11
  And I'm not going to take it back,
E♭m7(11)                        D♭5          A♭add11
  I'm not going to say I don't mean that,
E♭m7(11)                             D♭5     A♭add11
  You're the target that I'm aiming at,
            G♭add9         D♭*   A♭add11
And I'll get that mess - age home.
```

Verse 3

D♭ Fm♭6 A♭add11
My song is love,
D♭ Fm♭6 A♭add11 G♭add9
My song is love un - known
D♭ Fm♭6 A♭add11
And I'm on fire for you, clearly.

G♭add9 Fm♭6 A♭add11
You don't have___ to be___ a - lone.
G♭add9 Fm♭6 A♭add11
You don't have___ to be on your own.

Chorus 2

E♭m7(11) D♭5 A♭add11
And I'm not going to take it back,
E♭m7(11) D♭5 A♭add11
I'm not going to say I don't mean that,
E♭m7(11) D♭5 A♭add11
You're the target that I'm aiming at
G♭add9 D♭* A♭add11
And I'm nothing___ on my own,
G♭add9 D♭* A♭add11
Got to get that mes - sage home.

Instrumental 1 𝄆 E♭m7(11) | E♭m7(11) | D♭5 | A♭add11 𝄇

Chorus 3

E♭m7(11) D♭5 A♭add11
And I'm not going to stand and wait,
E♭m7(11) D♭5 A♭add11
Not going to leave it until it's much too late,
E♭m7(11) D♭5 A♭add11
On a platform I'm going to stand and say
G♭add9 D♭* A♭add11
That I'm nothing___ on my own,
G♭add9 D♭* A♭add11
And I love you, please come home.

Instrumental 2 𝄆 G♭add9 | D♭* | A♭add11 | B♭m7 𝄇

Outro

G♭add9 D♭* A♭add11 B♭m7
But my song is love, is love unknown
G♭add9 D♭* A♭add11 D♭*
And I've got to get___ that message home.

MOSES

Words & Music by
Guy Berryman, Jon Buckland, Will Champion & Chris Martin

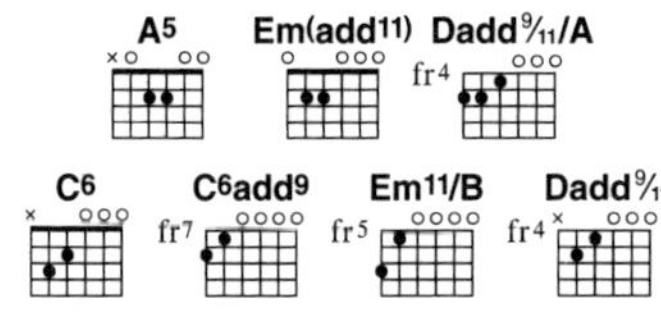

Capo second fret

Tune guitar (from bottom string): E, A, D, G, A, E

Intro ‖: **A5** | **Em(add11)** | **Em(add11)** | **Dadd9/11/A** :‖ *Play 4 times*

Verse 1

```
A5          Em(add11)
   Come  on  now
                     Dadd9/11/A
Don't you wanna see
A5       Em(add11)
   This thing that's
                  Dadd9/11/A
Happening to me?
A5       Em(add11)
   Like Moses
                     Dadd9/11/A
Has power over sea
A5     Em(add11)
   So you've got
                 Dadd9/11/A
A power over me.
```

Instrumental 1 ‖: **A5** | **Em(add11)** | **Em(add11)** | **Dadd9/11/A** :‖ *Play 4 times*

Verse 2

A5 Em(add11)
Come on now

Dadd9/11/A
Don't you want to know

A5 Em(add11)
That you're a refuge,

Dadd9/11/A
Somewhere I can go.

A5 Em(add11)
And you're air that,

Dadd9/11/A
Air that I can breathe.

A5 Em(add11)
You're my golden

Dadd9/11/A
Opportuni - ty.

Pre-chorus 1

C6
And oh,

C6add9 Em11/B Dadd9/11
Oh, yes I would

C6
If I only could.

C6add9 Em11/B Dadd9/11
Then you know I would.

Chorus 1

C6 Dadd9/11
Now baby I

C6 Dadd9/11
Oh, baby I.

Instrumental 2 ||: A5 | Em(add11) | Em(add11) | Dadd9/11/A :||

Verse 3

A5 Em(add11)
Come on now
Dadd9/11/A
Don't you wanna see
A5 Em(add11)
That just what a difference
Dadd9/11/A
You have made to me.
A5 Em(add11)
And I'll be waiting
Dadd9/11/A
No matter what you say
A5 Em(add11)
I'll keep waiting
Dadd9/11/A
For days and days and days.

Pre-chorus 2

C6
And oh,
C6add9 Em11/B Dadd9/11
Oh, yes I would
C6
If I only could.
C6add9 Em11/B Dadd9/11
And you know I would.

Chorus 2

C6 Dadd9/11
And baby I
C6 Dadd9/11
Oh baby I wish.

Bridge

‖: A5 | Em(add11) | Em(add11) | Dadd9/11/A :‖ *Play 4 times*
w/vocal ad libs.

C6 Dadd9/11 C6
If the skies go and fall down let it fall on me
Dadd9/11 C6
If you're caught in a break-down you can break on me
Dadd9/11 C6
If the sky's gonna fall down let it fall on me.
Dadd9/11
Oh Lord, let it fall on me.

Outro

‖: A5 | Em(add11) | Em(add11) | Dadd9/11/A :‖ *Play 3 times*

| C6 | Dadd9/11 | Em(add11) ‖

MURDER

Words & Music by
Guy Berryman, Jon Buckland, Will Champion & Chris Martin

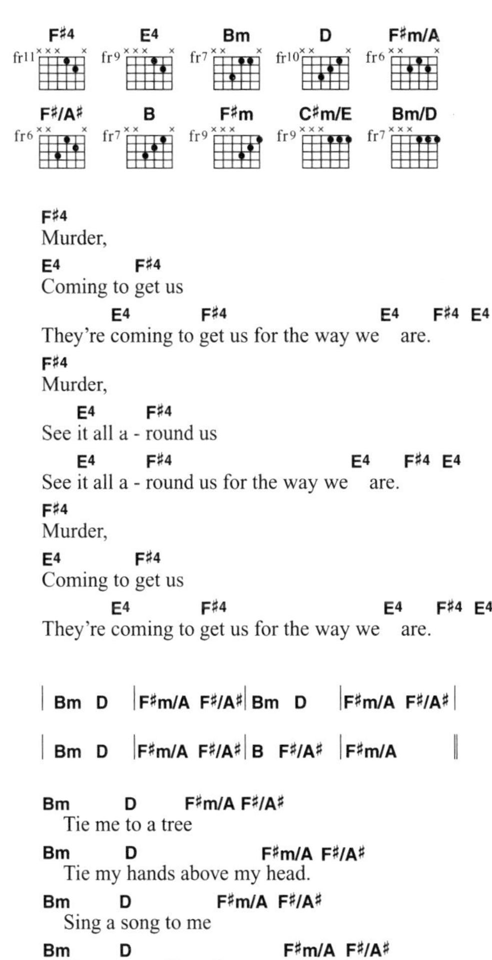

Intro

F♯4
Murder,
E4 F♯4
Coming to get us
E4 F♯4 E4 F♯4 E4
They're coming to get us for the way we are.
F♯4
Murder,
E4 F♯4
See it all a - round us
E4 F♯4 E4 F♯4 E4
See it all a - round us for the way we are.
F♯4
Murder,
E4 F♯4
Coming to get us
E4 F♯4 E4 F♯4 E4
They're coming to get us for the way we are.

Link 1

| Bm D | F♯m/A F♯/A♯ | Bm D | F♯m/A F♯/A♯ |

| Bm D | F♯m/A F♯/A♯ | B F♯/A♯ | F♯m/A ‖

Verse 1

Bm D F♯m/A F♯/A♯
Tie me to a tree
Bm D F♯m/A F♯/A♯
Tie my hands above my head.
Bm D F♯m/A F♯/A♯
Sing a song to me
Bm D F♯m/A F♯/A♯
Sing a song like what you said.

Link 2 | Bm D | F♯m/A F♯/A♯ | Bm D | F♯m/A F♯/A♯ ||

Oh...

Chorus 1

Bm D F♯m/A F♯/A♯
They're gonna murder me
Bm D F♯m/A F♯/A♯
They're gonna track me down.
Bm D F♯m/A F♯/A♯
And even be - fore I sleep
B F♯/A♯ F♯m/A
I cry mur - der.

Link 3 | F♯4 E4 | F♯4 E4 | F♯4 E4 | F♯4 E4 ||

Verse 2

Bm D F♯m/A F♯/A♯
Come spit at us
Bm D F♯m/A F♯/A♯
Come and throw your weight a - round.
Bm D F♯m/A F♯/A♯
Come and fight with us
Bm D F♯m/A F♯/A♯
Try and knock us to the ground.

Chorus 2

Bm D F♯m/A F♯/A♯
They're gonna murder me
Bm D F♯m/A F♯/A♯
They're gonna track me down.
Bm D F♯m/A F♯/A♯
And even be - fore I sleep
B F♯m/A F♯/A♯
I scream mur - der.

Bridge

F♯m C♯m/E Bm/D F♯m C♯m/E Bm/D
Murder...
F♯m C♯m/E Bm/D
Oh, now what can it possibly gain.
F♯m C♯m/E Bm/D
Oh, what could it possibly gain.
F♯m C♯m/E Bm/D
Oh, what could it possibly gain.
F♯m C♯m/E Bm/D
Oh, yeah what could it possibly gain.

Link 4 | Bm D | F♯m/A F♯/A♯ | Bm D | F♯m/A F♯/A♯ |

w/vocal ad libs.

| Bm D | F♯m/A F♯/A♯ | F♯m/A | F♯m/A ||

Outro | F♯4 E4 | F♯4 E4 | F♯4 E4 | F♯4 E4 |

```
F♯4
Murder,
E4          F♯4
Coming to get us
          E4          F♯4                           E4     F♯4  E4
They're coming to get us for the way we    are.
F♯4
Murder,
    E4        F♯4
See it all a - round us
    E4        F♯4                              E4     F♯4  E4
See it all a - round us for the way we    are.
F♯4
Murder,
E4          F♯4
Coming to get us
          E4          F♯4                           E4     F♯4  E4
They're coming to get us for the way we    are.
F♯4
Murder,
N.C.
See it all around you.

See it all around you and the way we are.
```

NO MORE KEEPING MY FEET ON THE GROUND

Words & Music by
Guy Berryman, Jon Buckland, Will Champion & Chris Martin

Bmadd11 (fr7) F♯m11 E Badd11 (fr7) F♯11 Aadd9 (fr5)

Intro |: Bmadd11 | Bmadd11 F♯m11 | E | E :| *Play 4 times*

| Badd11 | Badd11 | Badd11 | Badd11 ||

Verse 1

```
Badd11
Sometimes I wake up when I'm falling asleep,

I think that maybe the curtains, are closing on me,
             F♯m11                Badd11
But I wake up, yes I wake up smiling.
```

Verse 2

```
Badd11
Sometimes I feel the chance is surprising,

Surprisingly good to be moving around,
            F♯m11                Badd11
So I wake up, yes I wake up smiling.
```

Chorus 1

```
   E
So what, I feel fine,
      F♯11
I'm okay, I've seen the lighter side of life
      E
I'm alright, I feel good,
        F♯11
So I'll go, I'll try to start moving.
```

| Badd11 | Badd11 | Badd11 | Badd11 ||

Verse 3

Badd11
Sometimes I wake up and I'm falling asleep,
F♯m11
But I've got to get going, so much that I wanted to do,
Badd11 Aadd9
But I wake up smiling.

Bridge 1

F♯11
And this could be my last chance,
Aadd9
Of saving my innocence,
F♯11
And this could be my last chance,
Badd11
No more keeping my feet on the ground.

| Badd11 | Badd11 | Badd11 ||

Verse 4

Badd11
Sometimes I feel the chance is surprising,

Surprisingly good to be moving around,
F♯m11 Badd11
And I move, and I wake up smiling.

Chorus 2

E
So what, I feel fine,
F♯11
I feel okay, I've seen the lighter side of life
E
I'm alright, I feel good,
F♯11 Aadd9
So I'll go, well it's time to start moving.

Bridge 2

As Bridge 1

Outro

Badd11
And there's nothing to keep them,

There's nothing to keep them down

And there's nothing to keep them,

There's nothing to keep them down.

| Badd11 | Badd11 ||

ONE I LOVE

Words & Music by
Guy Berryman, Jon Buckland, Will Champion & Chris Martin

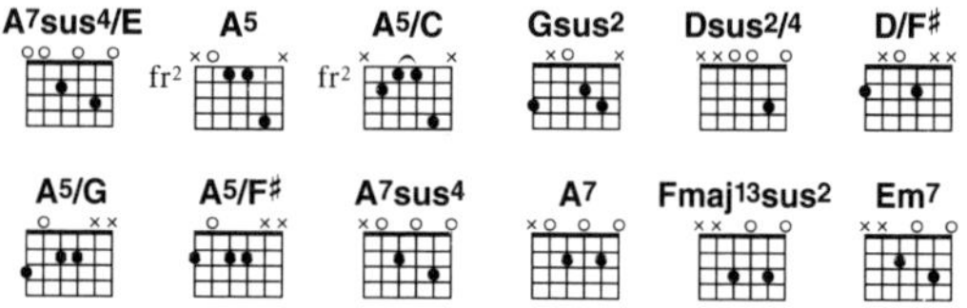

A7sus4/E　A5 (fr2)　A5/C (fr2)　Gsus2　Dsus2/4　D/F♯

A5/G　A5/F♯　A7sus4　A7　Fmaj13sus2　Em7

Intro

| A7sus4/E |

x4
|: A5 | A5/C | Gsus2 | Dsus2/4 :|

| A5 | Gsus2 D/F♯ | A5 | Gsus2 D/F♯ ||

Verse 1

A5 Gsus2 D/F♯
Could you, could you come back?
A5 Gsus2 D/F♯
Come back together
A5 Gsus2 D/F♯
Put yourself on the band
A5 Gsus2 D/F♯
And see us forever.
A5 Gsus2 D/F♯
Could you, could you come home?
A5 Gsus2 D/F♯
Come home forever,
A5 Gsus2 D/F♯
Surely things in the band
A5 Gsus2 D/F♯
Keep us together.

Chorus 1

| A5 | A5/C | Gsus2 | Dsus2/4 |
'Cause you're the one I love
| A5 | A5/C | Gsus2 | Dsus2/4 |
You're the one I love
| A5 | A5/C | Gsus2 | Dsus2/4 |
You're the one I love
| A5 | A5/C | Gsus2 | Dsus2/4 |
Ah, ah.

Link 1 |: A5 | A5/C | Gsus2 | Dsus2/4 :| x2

Verse 2

A5 Gsus2 D/F♯
Could you, could you come in?
A5 Gsus2 D/F♯
Could you tell me wherever?
A5 Gsus2 D/F♯
Tie yourself to a mast
A5 Gsus2 D/F♯
It's now or it's never.
A5 Gsus2 D/F♯
Could it tear us apart?
A5 Gsus2 D/F♯
It'll soon be forever
A5 Gsus2 D/F♯
It's gonna tear us apart
A5 Gsus2 D/F♯
Keep us together.

Chorus 2

| A5 | A5/C | Gsus2 | Dsus2/4 |
You're the one I love
| A5 | A5/C | Gsus2 | Dsus2/4 |
You're the one I love
| A5 | A5/C | Gsus2 | Dsus2/4 |
Ah. Ah. You're the one I love
| A5 | A5/C | Gsus2 | Dsus2/4 |
The one I love.

Link 2

|: A5 | A5 | A5 | A5 :|
Oooooooooo
| A5 | A5 | A5/G | A5/F♯ |
Oooooooooo.

Outro

|: A5 | A5/C | Gsus2 | Dsus2/4 :| x4
|: A7sus4 | A7sus4 | A7 | A7 :| x2
|: Fmaj13sus2 | Em7 | A7 | A7 :| x3
| Fmaj13sus2 | Em7 | A7 ||

ONLY SUPERSTITION

Words & Music by
Guy Berryman, Jon Buckland, Will Champion & Chris Martin

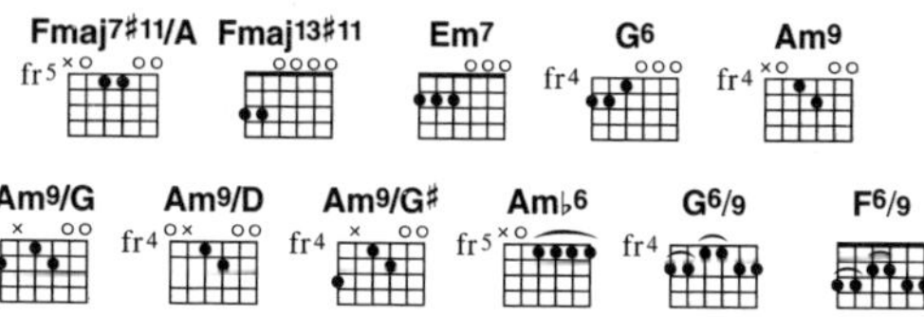

Tune guitar (from bottom string): D, A, C, G, B, E

Intro | Fmaj7♯11/A | Fmaj7♯11/A |

|: Fmaj13♯11 Em7 Fmaj13♯11 | G6 :| *Play 4 times*

Verse 1

Am9 Am9/G Am9/D Am9/G
The cardboard head I see

Am9 Am9/G Am9/D Am9/G
Has found its way to me,

Am9 Am9/G Am9/D Am9/G
It's out and it's out and it's out,

Am9 Am9/G Am9/D Am9/G
Making me cry.

Am9 Am9/G Am9/D Am9/G
I sleep but I will not move,

Am9 Am9/G Am9/D Am9/G
I'm too scared to leave my room,

Am9 Am9/G Am9/D Am9/G Am9 Am9/G Am9/D Am9/G
But I won't be defeated, oh no.

Chorus 1

Fmaj13♯11 G6 Fmaj13♯11
What if cars don't go my way

G6 Fmaj13♯11
And it's sure to spoil my day?

G6 Fmaj13♯11 G6
But in voices loud and clear you say to me;

Chorus 1

Fmaj13#11 G6 Fmaj13#11
What if cars don't go my way

G6 Fmaj13#11
And it's sure to spoil my day?

G6 Fmaj13#11 G6
But in voices loud and clear you say to me;

Fmaj13#11 Em7 G6
"It's only superstition,

Em7 Fmaj13#11 G6 Fmaj13#11 Em7 G6
It's only your imagination,

Em7 Fmaj13#11 G6 Fmaj13#11 Em7
It's only all the things that you fear

Fmaj13#11 G6 Em7 Fmaj13#11 G6
And the things from which you can't escape."

| Fmaj13#11 Em7 Fmaj13#11 | G6 Em7 Fmaj13#11 G6 ||

Verse 2

Am9 Am9/G Am9/D Am9/G
Keep clean for the thousandth time,

Am9 Am9/G Am9/D Am9/G
Stand still and wait in line,

Am9 Am9/G Am9/D Am9/G
Some numbers are better than others,

Am9 Am9/G Am9/D Am9/G
Oh no.

Chorus 2

Fmaj13#11 G6 Fmaj13#11
What if cars don't go my way

G6 Fmaj13#11
And it's sure to spoil my day?

G6 Fmaj13#11 G6
But in voices loud and clear you say to me;

Fmaj13#11 Em7 G6
"It's only superstition,

Em7 Fmaj13#11 G6 Fmaj13#11 Em7 G6
It's only your imagination,

Em7 Fmaj13#11 G6 Fmaj13#11 Em7
It's only all of the things that you fear

Fmaj13#11 G6 Em7 Fmaj13#11 G6
And the things which you cannot ex - plain."

| Fmaj13♯11 Em7 Fmaj13♯11 | G6 Em7 Fmaj13♯11 G6 ||

Bridge

```
Fmaj13♯11                 G6  Am9/G♯                Am9
   And it's making me cry,   and it's making me cry,
Fmaj13♯11               G6  Am9/G♯                Am9
   And I'm slipping away,   and I'm slipping away.
```

Coda

```
Am♭6                G6/9                      F6/9
   It's only superstition, only your imagination,
Am♭6                G6/9                F6/9
   It's only superstition, only superstition.
```

PARACHUTES

Words & Music by
Guy Berryman, Jon Buckland, Will Champion & Chris Martin

B G♯m F♯m E

Tune guitar (from bottom string): E, A, B, G, B, D♯

Intro | B | G♯m | B | G♯m |
| F♯m | F♯m | E | E ||

Verse 1
```
B
   In a haze,
  G♯m
A stormy haze,
B
   I'll be 'round,
        G♯m            F♯m
I'll be loving you always,
  E
Always
```

Verse 2
```
B
   Here I am
          G♯m
And I'll take my time.
B
   Here I am
          G♯m             F♯m
And I'll wait in line always,
  E
Always.
```

POLITIK

Words & Music by
Guy Berryman, Jon Buckland, Will Champion & Chris Martin

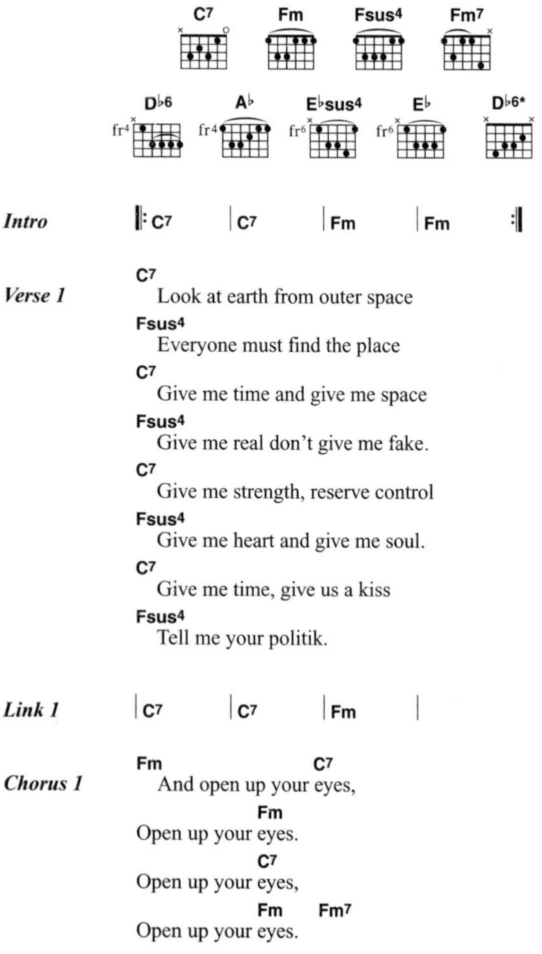


```
Intro      ||: C7      | C7      | Fm      | Fm      :||

           C7
Verse 1       Look at earth from outer space
           Fsus4
              Everyone must find the place
           C7
              Give me time and give me space
           Fsus4
              Give me real don't give me fake.
           C7
              Give me strength, reserve control
           Fsus4
              Give me heart and give me soul.
           C7
              Give me time, give us a kiss
           Fsus4
              Tell me your politik.

Link 1     | C7      | C7      | Fm      |

           Fm                 C7
Chorus 1      And open up your eyes,
                          Fm
           Open up your eyes.
                          C7
           Open up your eyes,
                          Fm      Fm7
           Open up your eyes.
```

Verse 2

C7
Give me one, 'cause one is best,
Fsus4
In confusion confidence
C7
Give me peace of mind, and trust
Fsus4
And don't forget the rest of us.
C7
Give me strength, reserve control
Fsus4
Give me heart and give me soul.
C7
Wounds that heal, and cracks that fix
Fsus4
Tell me your politik.

Chorus 2

                                        C7
And open up your eyes,
                                Fm
Open up your eyes.
                                C7
Open up your eyes,
                                Fm
Open up your eyes.
        Fm7   C7
Just open up your (eyes.)

Link 2

| C7 | C7 | Fm | Fm | D♭6 |
eyes.

| D♭6 | A♭ | A♭ | E♭sus4 | E♭ ||

Outro

Fm   D♭6*   A♭   E♭sus4   E♭   Fm
Give me love over, love over, love over this.   Ah. ______
                                D♭6*   A♭   E♭sus4   E♭
Give me love over, love over, love over this.   Ah, ah ______

| Fm | Fm | D♭6* | D♭6* | A♭ | A♭ |

| E♭sus4 | E♭ | Fm | Fm | D♭6* | D♭6* |

| A♭ | A♭ | E♭sus4 | E♭ | Fm (fermata) ||

POUR ME (LIVE)

Words & Music by
Guy Berryman, Jon Buckland, Will Champion & Chris Martin

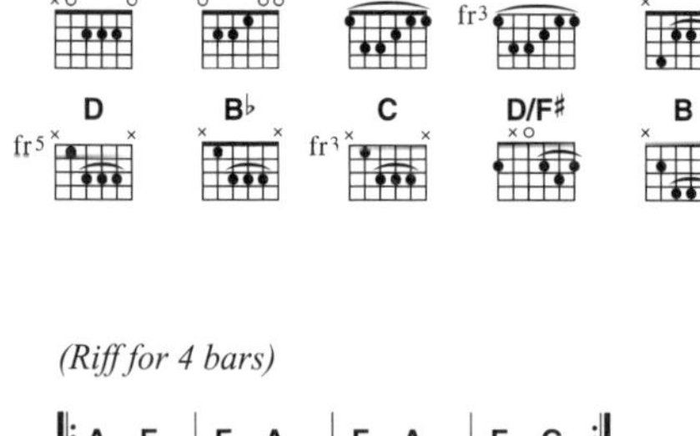

(Riff for 4 bars)

```
Intro      |: A  E  | F  A  | F  A  | F  G  :|

           A     E F              A
Verse 1       Pour me flowing out to sea
               F         A           F  G
           An opportu - nity that went by.
           A        E       F           A
              Pour you now what you gonna do
               F                  A           F  G
           Now what you gonna do you just cry.


Link 1     | A  E  | F  A  | F  A  | F  G  ||

           A        E     F            A
Verse 2       Pour me so blind I couldn't see
                 F        A
           The forest for the trees
                           F  G
           I don't know why.
           A        E        F           A
              Pour you, you split yourself in two
               F                  A           F  G
           Now what you gonna do you just cry.
```

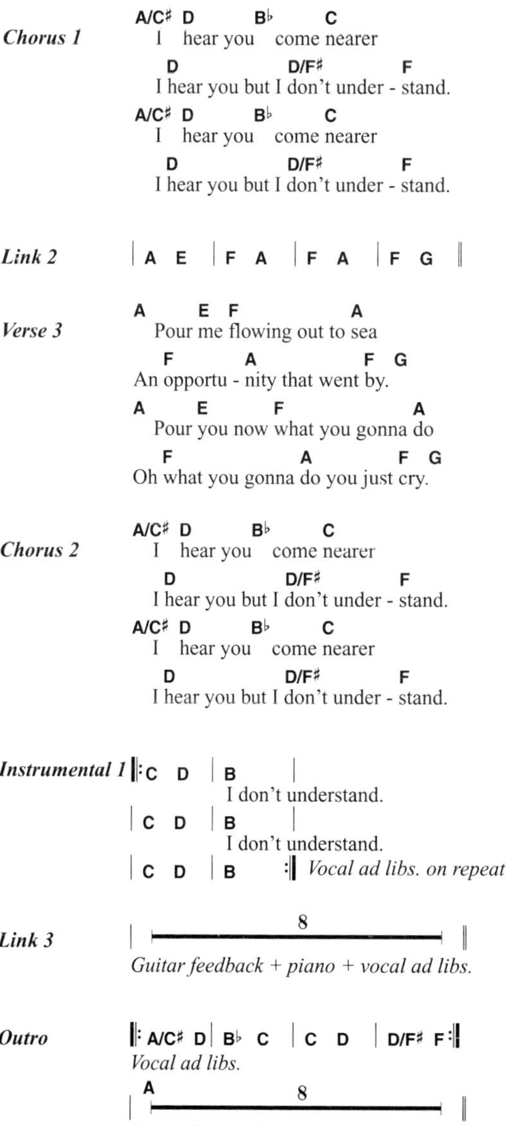

Chorus 1

A/C♯ D Bb C
I hear you come nearer
D D/F♯ F
I hear you but I don't under - stand.
A/C♯ D Bb C
I hear you come nearer
D D/F♯ F
I hear you but I don't under - stand.

Link 2

| A E | F A | F A | F G ||

Verse 3

A E F A
Pour me flowing out to sea
F A F G
An opportu - nity that went by.
A E F A
Pour you now what you gonna do
F A F G
Oh what you gonna do you just cry.

Chorus 2

A/C♯ D Bb C
I hear you come nearer
D D/F♯ F
I hear you but I don't under - stand.
A/C♯ D Bb C
I hear you come nearer
D D/F♯ F
I hear you but I don't under - stand.

Instrumental 1

||: C D | B |
I don't understand.
| C D | B |
I don't understand.
| C D | B :|| *Vocal ad libs. on repeat*

Link 3

| 8 ||
Guitar feedback + piano + vocal ad libs.

Outro

||: A/C♯ D | Bb C | C D | D/F♯ F :||
Vocal ad libs.
A
| 8 ||
Guitar feedback + piano

PROOF

Words & Music by
Guy Berryman, Jon Buckland, Will Champion & Chris Martin

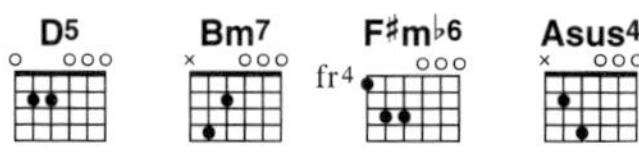

Capo second fret
Tune guitar (from bottom string): D, G, C, A, A, D

Intro | D5 | Bm7 | D5 | Bm7 ||

Verse 1

```
D5                Bm7
   So I waited for you
F♯m♭6               Bm7
   What wouldn't I do?
D5                     Bm7
   And I'm covered it's true
F♯m♭6             Bm7
   I'm covered in you.
D5                Bm7
   If I ever want proof
F♯m♭6        Bm7
   I find it in you.
D5                 Bm7
   Yeah I honestly do
F♯m♭6           Bm7
   In you I find proof.
```

Chorus 1

```
Asus4        Bm7
   Light dark
F♯m♭6          Bm7
   Bright spark.
Asus4        Bm7
   Light dark    and then
F♯m♭6     Bm7
   Light.
```

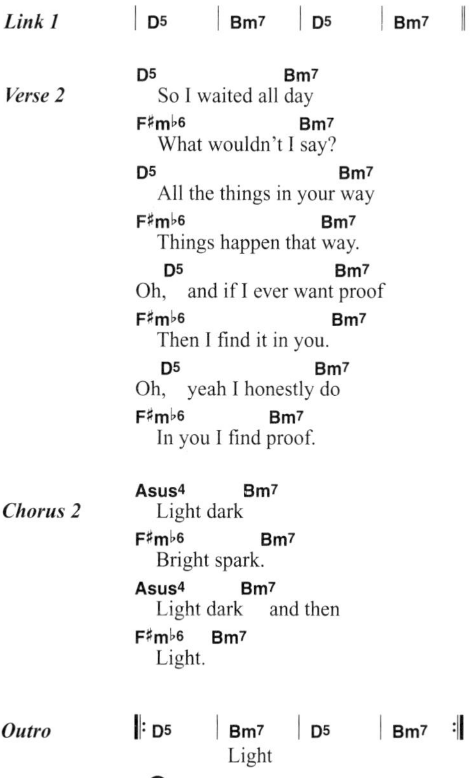

Link 1 | D5 | Bm7 | D5 | Bm7 ||

Verse 2

```
D5                    Bm7
   So I waited all day
F♯m♭6                   Bm7
   What wouldn't I say?
D5                              Bm7
   All the things in your way
F♯m♭6                      Bm7
   Things happen that way.
    D5                       Bm7
Oh,    and if I ever want proof
F♯m♭6                        Bm7
   Then I find it in you.
    D5                    Bm7
Oh,    yeah I honestly do
F♯m♭6               Bm7
   In you I find proof.
```

Chorus 2

```
Asus4        Bm7
   Light dark
F♯m♭6            Bm7
   Bright spark.
Asus4        Bm7
   Light dark     and then
F♯m♭6     Bm7
   Light.
```

Outro |: D5 | Bm7 | D5 | Bm7 :|
Light

| D5 (fermata) ||

A RUSH OF BLOOD TO THE HEAD

Words & Music by
Guy Berryman, Jon Buckland, Will Champion & Chris Martin

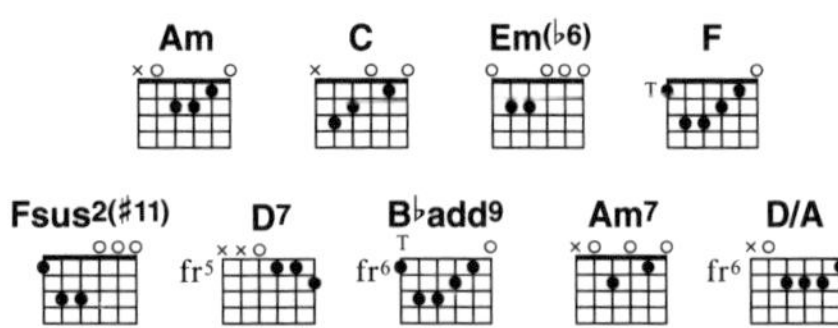

Tune guitar (from bottom string): E, A, D, G, B, C

Verse 1

```
                Am                                          C
He said I'm gonna buy this place and burn it down,
  Em(♭6)                                      Am
I'm gonna put it six feet underground.
                                                            C
He said I'm gonna buy this place and watch it fall
   Em(♭6)                                                    Am
Stand here beside me baby in the crumbling walls.
```

Verse 2

```
           Am                                     C
Oh I'm gonna buy this place and start a fire,
   Em(♭6)                                           Am
Stand here until I fill all your heart's desires.
                                                         C
Because I'm gonna buy this place and see it burn
  Em(♭6)                                      Am   | Am   |
Do back the things it did to you in return.
```

Link 1

```
      F        Fsus2(♯11)
Ha _ ha ________
      F        Fsus2(♯11)
Ha _ ha.________
```

```
                     Am                                  C
Verse 3      He said I'm gonna buy a gun and start a war,
              Em(♭6)                                       Am
             If you can tell me something worth fighting for.
                                                         C
             Oh and I'm gonna buy this place, is what I say,
             Em(♭6)                                  Am | Am |
             Blame it upon a rush of blood to the head.

                 F                                           D7
Chorus 1     Honey, all the movements you're starting to make
                                                 F
             See me crumble and fall on my face.
                                                     D7
             And I know the mistakes that I've made,
                       B♭add9                  F
             See it all disappear without a trace,
                                                 D7
             And they call as they beckon you on,
                           B♭add9                  (Am)
             They said start as you mean to go on.

             | Am       | C        | Em(♭6)   |

             Am
               Start as you mean to go on.

             | Am       | C        | Em(♭6)   | Am       |

                     Am                                    C
Verse 4      He said I'm gonna buy this place and see it go,
               Em(♭6)                                        Am
             Stand here beside my baby, watch the orange glow.
                                                     C
             Some will laugh and some just sit and cry,
                  Em(♭6)                                       Am
             But you just sit down there and you wonder why.

                  Am                               C
Verse 5      So I'm gonna buy a gun and start a war,
             Em(♭6)                                       Am
             If you can tell me something worth fighting for.
                                                         C
             Oh and I'm gonna buy this place, is what I say,
             Em(♭6)                                  Am
             Blame it upon a rush of blood to the head, oh to the head.
```

```
           F                                         D7
Chorus 2   Honey, all the movements you're starting to make
                                         F
           See me crumble and fall on my face.
                                               D7
           And I know the mistakes that I've made,
                  B♭add9               F
           See it all disappear without a tracc,
                                             D7
           And they call as they beckon you on,
                     B♭add9                  (Am)
           They said start as you mean to go on.
            Am    C                  Em(♭6)
                   As you mean to go on,
           Am
              As you mean to go on.

           | Am      | C        | Em(♭6)   |


           Am
Verse 6      So meet me by the bridge,
                                   C
           Oh meet me by the lake.
                               Em(♭6)               Am
           When am I gonna see that pretty face again?

           Oh meet me on the road,
                                C
           Oh meet me where I ___ said,
                           Em(♭6)                Am7     D/A
           Blame it all upon a rush of blood to the head.


Outro      | Am7  D/A | Am7  D/A | Am7  D/A | Am (fermata)     ||
```

SPEED OF SOUND

Words & Music by
Guy Berryman, Jon Buckland, Will Champion & Chris Martin

Asus4 Em7 D G
A Bm7 F♯m D5 E

Intro ‖: Asus4 | Em7 | Em7 | D :‖

Verse 1

```
       Asus4            Em7
How long before I get in?
                          D
Before it starts, before I be - gin?
       Asus4              Em7
How long before you de - cide?
                          D
Before I know what it feels like?
         Asus4       Em7
Where to, where do I go?
                                 D
If you never try then you'll never know,
       Asus4          Em7
How long do I have to climb
                                  D
Up on the side of this mountain of mine?
```

Instrumental 1 ‖: Asus4 | Em7 | Em7 | D :‖

Verse 2

```
        Asus4        Em7
Look up, I look up at night,
                                  D
Planets are moving at the speed of light.
         Asus4      Em7
Climb up, up in the trees,
                                                D
Every chance that you get is a chance you seize.
       Asus4          Em7
How long am I gonna stand
```

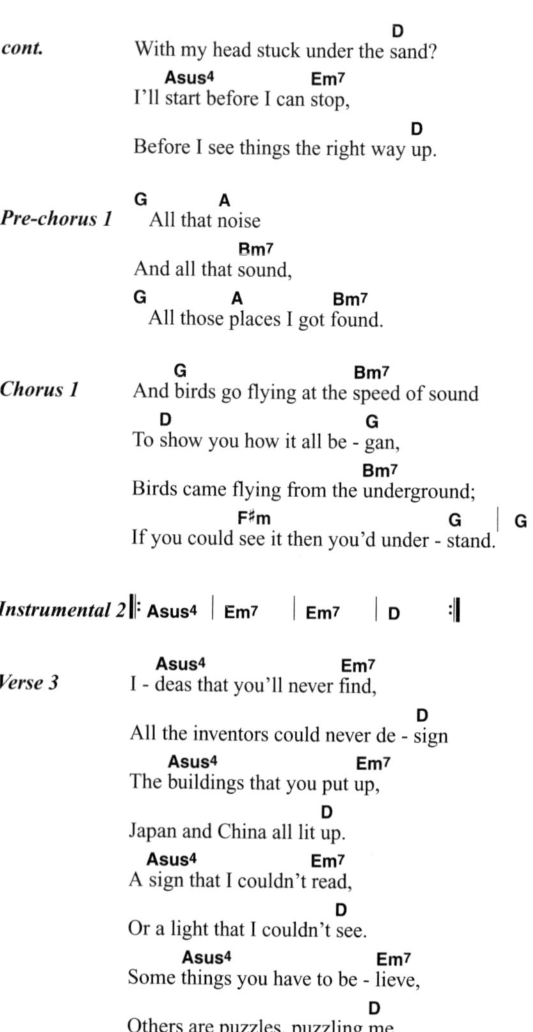

```
                                              D
cont.             With my head stuck under the sand?
                     Asus4             Em7
                  I'll start before I can stop,
                                                D
                  Before I see things the right way up.

                  G         A
Pre-chorus 1        All that noise
                              Bm7
                  And all that sound,
                  G            A            Bm7
                    All those places I got found.

                     G                       Bm7
Chorus 1          And birds go flying at the speed of sound
                    D                      G
                  To show you how it all be - gan,
                                             Bm7
                  Birds came flying from the underground;
                              F#m                     G  | G |
                  If you could see it then you'd under - stand.

Instrumental 2 |: Asus4 | Em7 | Em7 | D :|

                    Asus4                 Em7
Verse 3           I - deas that you'll never find,
                                                D
                  All the inventors could never de - sign
                      Asus4               Em7
                  The buildings that you put up,
                                        D
                  Japan and China all lit up.
                    Asus4             Em7
                  A sign that I couldn't read,
                                          D
                  Or a light that I couldn't see.
                       Asus4                  Em7
                  Some things you have to be - lieve,
                                              D
                  Others are puzzles, puzzling me.
```

Pre-chorus 2

```
G        A
All that noise
                 Bm7
And all that sound,
G          A             Bm7
All those places I got found.
```

Chorus 2

```
    G                          Bm7
And birds go flying at the speed of sound
   D                          G
To show you how it all be - gan,
                               Bm7
Birds came flying from the underground;
                F♯m                     G
If you could see it then you'd under - stand,
                 F♯m                      G    | G   |
Ah, when you see it then you'll under - stand.
```

Instrumental 3

```
| D     | D     | D     | D     |
| D     | D     | D5    | D5    ||
```

Pre-chorus 3

```
G         A                          Bm7
All those signs, I knew what they meant,
                      E
Some things you can't invent,
G         A                    Bm7     E
Some get made and some get sent, ooh.___
```

Chorus 3

```
    G                          Bm7
And birds go flying at the speed of sound
   D                          G
To show you how it all be - gan,
                               Bm7
Birds came flying from the underground,
                F♯m                     G
If you could see it then you'd under - stand.
                 F♯m                      G
Ah, when you see it then you'll under - stand.

| G     | G     | G     | G     ||
```

SEE YOU SOON

Words & Music by
Guy Berryman, Jon Buckland, Will Champion & Chris Martin

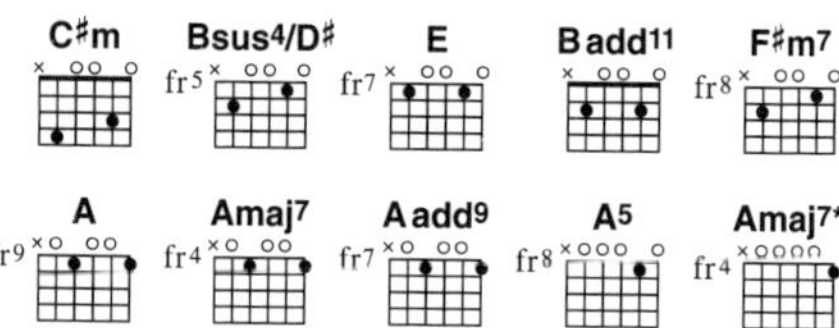

Tune guitar (from bottom string): F♯, G, D, D, B, D,
Capo second fret

Intro | C♯m Bsus4/D♯ E | Badd11 | C♯m Bsus4/D♯ E | Badd11 |
| C♯m Bsus4/D♯ E | Badd11 | F♯m7 E | Badd11 ||

Verse 1

```
C♯m  Bsus4/D♯  E           Badd11
  So you       lost your trust,
                        C♯m
And you never shared her,
     Bsus4/D♯  E          Badd11
And you      never shared her.
C♯m   Bsus4/D♯  E            Badd11
  But don't     break your back,
                C♯m    Bsus4/D♯  E        Badd11
If you ever see this,  don't     answer that.
```

Chorus 1

```
A       Amaj7  Aadd9  Amaj7
  In a bullet - proof vest,
              Badd11     A
With the windows all closed,
          Amaj7   Aadd9  Amaj7             A5
I'll be doing    my      best, I'll see you soon
A        Amaj7   Aadd9   Amaj7
  In a tele  -   scope   lens.
                Badd11       A5        Amaj7*
And when all you want is friends,  I'll see you soon.
```

Link 1 | C♯m Bsus4/D♯ E | Badd11 | C♯m Bsus4/D♯ E | Badd11 ||

Verse 2

C♯m Bsus4/D♯ E Badd11
So they came for you,
C♯m
They came snapping at your heels,
Bsus4/D♯ E Badd11
They come snapping at your heels.
C♯m Bsus4/D♯ E Badd11
But don't break your back,
C♯m
If you ever say this,
Bsus4/D♯ E Badd11
But don't answer that.

Chorus 2

A Amaj7 Aadd9 Amaj7
In a bullet - proof vest,
Badd11 A
With the windows all closed,
Amaj7 Aadd9 Amaj7 A5
I'll bc doing my best, I'll see you soon
A Amaj7 Aadd9 Amaj7
In a tele - scope lens.
Badd11 A5 Amaj7*
And when all you want is friends, I'll see you soon.

Link 2

| C♯m Bsus4/D♯ E | Badd11 | C♯m Bsus4/D♯ E | Badd11 |
I'll see you soon.

| C♯m Bsus4/D♯ E | Badd11 | C♯m Bsus4/D♯ E | Badd11 ||

Coda

A5 E Badd11
I know you lost your trust,
A5 E Badd11
I know you lost your trust,
A5 E Badd11
I know, don't lose your trust,
A5 E Badd11
I know you lost your trust.

THE SCIENTIST

Words & Music by
Guy Berryman, Jon Buckland, Will Champion & Chris Martin

Dm7 B♭ F Fsus2 C/F C C/G

Intro ‖: Dm7 | B♭ | F | Fsus2 :‖

Verse 1

Dm7 B♭
Come up to meet you,
F
Tell you I'm sorry,
Fsus2
You don't know how lovely you are.
Dm7 B♭
I had to find you,
F
Tell you I need you,
Fsus2 C/F
Tell you I'll set you apart.
Dm7 B♭
Tell me your secrets,
F
And ask me your questions,
Fsus2 C/F
Oh let's go back to the start.
Dm7 B♭
Running in circles,
F
Coming up tails,
Fsus2 C/F
Heads on a silence apart.

Chorus 1

B♭
Nobody said it was easy,
F Fsus2
It's such a shame for us to part.
B♭
Nobody said it was easy,
F C/F Fsus2 C
No-one ever said it would be this hard.
C/G (F)
Oh, take me back to the start.

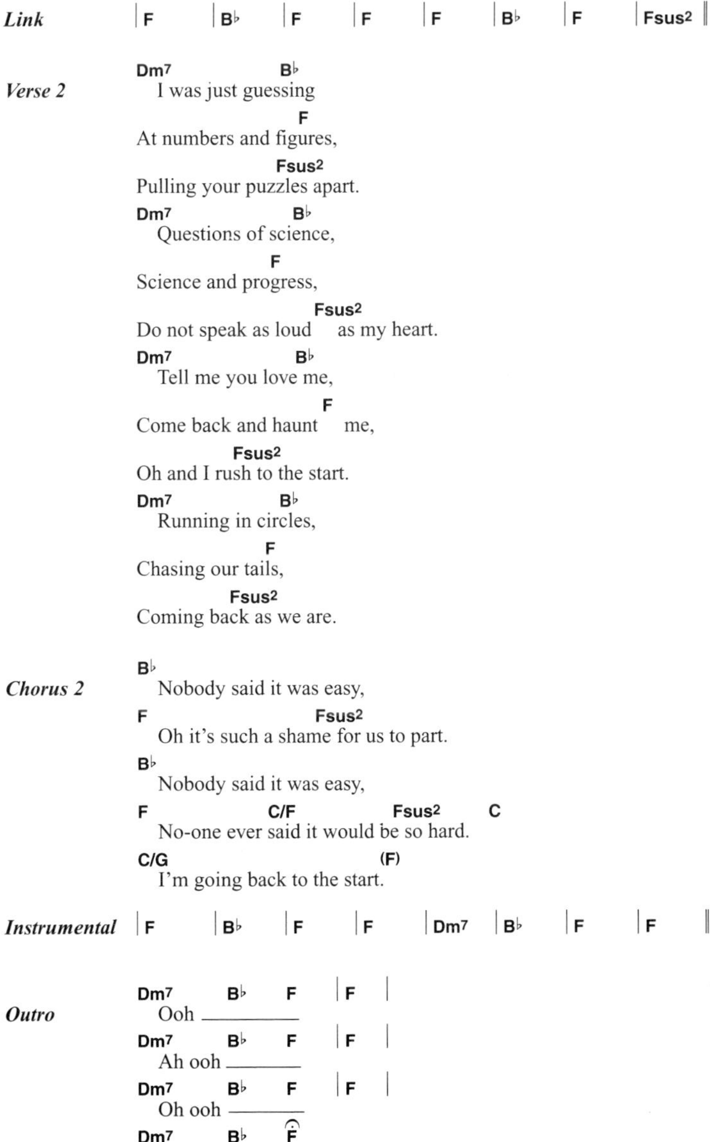

Link | F | B♭ | F | F | F | B♭ | F | Fsus2 ||

Verse 2

Dm7 B♭
I was just guessing
F
At numbers and figures,
Fsus2
Pulling your puzzles apart.
Dm7 B♭
Questions of science,
F
Science and progress,
Fsus2
Do not speak as loud as my heart.
Dm7 B♭
Tell me you love me,
F
Come back and haunt me,
Fsus2
Oh and I rush to the start.
Dm7 B♭
Running in circles,
F
Chasing our tails,
Fsus2
Coming back as we are.

Chorus 2

B♭
Nobody said it was easy,
F Fsus2
Oh it's such a shame for us to part.
B♭
Nobody said it was easy,
F C/F Fsus2 C
No-one ever said it would be so hard.
C/G (F)
I'm going back to the start.

Instrumental | F | B♭ | F | F | Dm7 | B♭ | F | F ||

Outro

Dm7 B♭ F | F |
Ooh ______
Dm7 B♭ F | F |
Ah ooh ______
Dm7 B♭ F | F |
Oh ooh ______
Dm7 B♭ F𝄐
Oh ooh.

SHIVER

Words & Music by
Guy Berryman, Jon Buckland, Will Champion & Chris Martin

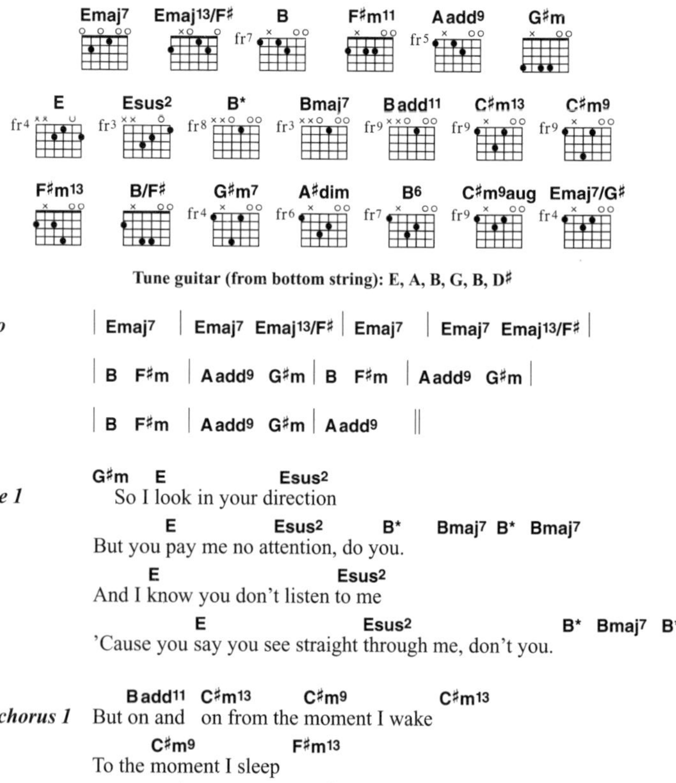

Tune guitar (from bottom string): E, A, B, G, B, D♯

Intro

| Emaj7 | Emaj7 Emaj13/F♯ | Emaj7 | Emaj7 Emaj13/F♯ |

| B F♯m | Aadd9 G♯m | B F♯m | Aadd9 G♯m |

| B F♯m | Aadd9 G♯m | Aadd9 ||

Verse 1

G♯m E Esus2
So I look in your direction
E Esus2 B* Bmaj7 B* Bmaj7
But you pay me no attention, do you.
E Esus2
And I know you don't listen to me
E Esus2 B* Bmaj7 B*
'Cause you say you see straight through me, don't you.

Pre-chorus 1

Badd11 C♯m13 C♯m9 C♯m13
But on and on from the moment I wake
C♯m9 F♯m13
To the moment I sleep
B/F♯ F♯m13
I'll be there by your side,
B/F♯ C♯m13
Just you try and stop me.
B G♯m7
I'll be waiting in line just to see if you care, oh whoa.

cont.

A♯dim B6
Did you want me to change?

A♯dim G♯m7
Well I'd change for good.

A♯dim B6
And I want you to know

C♯m9aug B6
That you'll always get your way.

A♯dim G♯m7 Emaj7/G♯
I wanted to say;

Chorus 1

B F♯m11 Aadd9 G♯m
Don't you shiver,

B6 F♯m11 Aadd9 G♯m
Shiver,

B Aadd9 G♯m7
Shiver, ooh. ______

Aadd9 G♯m
I'll always be waiting for you.

Verse 2

E Esus2
So you know how much I need you

E Esus2 B* Bmaj7 B* Bmaj7
But you never even see me, do you?

E Esus2 E Esus2 B* Bmaj7 B*
And is this my final chance of getting you?

Pre-chorus 2

Badd11 C♯m13 C♯m9 C♯m13
But on and on from the moment I wake

C♯m9 F♯m13
To the moment I sleep

B/F♯ F♯m13
I'll be there by your side,

B/F♯ C♯m13
Just you try and stop me.

B G♯m7
I'll be waiting in line just to see if you care, oh whoa.

A♯dim B6
Did you want me to change?

A♯dim G♯m7
Well I'd change for good.

A♯dim B6
And I want you to know

C♯m9aug B6
That you'll always get your way.

A♯dim G♯m7 Emaj7/G♯
I wanted to say;

Chorus 2

B F♯m11 Aadd9 G♯m
Don't you shiver,

B6 F♯m11 Aadd9 G♯m
Shiver,

B Aadd9 G♯m7
Shiver, ooh. ______

Aadd9 G♯m
I'll always be waiting for you.

| Emaj7 | Emaj7 | Emaj7 ||

Bridge

B Aadd9 Emaj7
Yeah, I'll always be waiting for you,

B Aadd9 Emaj7
Yeah, I'll always be waiting for you,

B Aadd9 Emaj7
Yeah, I'll always be waiting for you,

For you, I will always be waiting.

B F♯m11 Aadd9 G♯m
And it's you I see but you don't see me,

B F♯m11 Aadd9 G♯m
And it's you I hear so loud and clear.

B F♯m11 Aadd9 G♯m
I sing it loud ___ and clear

Aadd9 G♯m
And I'll always be waiting for you.

Verse 3

Emaj7 Esus2
So I look in your direction

Emaj7 Esus2
But you pay me no attention.

Emaj7 Esus2
And you know how much I need you

Emaj7 Esus2
But you never even see me.

SLEEPING SUN

Words & Music by
Guy Berryman, Jon Buckland, Will Champion & Chris Martin

A Asus4 Em7 G D/F♯ A7sus4 Cadd9 Cadd9/G

Capo sixth fret

Intro |: A | Asus4 | Asus4 | A :|

Verse 1

```
A                 Em7
Climb up your mountain
G              D/F♯
Nineteen and counting
A               Em7
You have got seven,
G          D/F♯
I have got one
A              Em      G            D/F♯
Blinded and hurting, misun - de - serving
A              Em7
I've got my secrets
G              D/F♯
You've only got the sleeping sun
```

Instrumental 1 | A | Asus4 | Asus4 | A ||

Verse 2

A Em7
When you've got a secret

G D/F♯
Then you've got to keep it

A Em7
When you've got a question

G D/F♯
Answers will come

A Em
Running and hiding

G D/F♯
Take and di - viding

A Em7
You've got your secrets

G D/F♯
I've only got a sleeping sun

Instrumental 2 ‖: A | Asus4 | Asus4 | A :‖

Chorus 1

A A7sus4
Singing, ooh, ooh, ooh

A A7sus4
Ooh, ooh, ooh

A A7sus4
Ooh, ooh, ooh

A A7sus4
Ooh, ooh, ooh

A A7sus4
Ah, ah, ah

A A7sus4
Oh, oh, oh

A A7sus4
Ah, ah, ah

A A7sus4
Oh, oh, oh

Instrumental 3 | A | A | A | A ‖

Verse 3

```
A              Em7
And you, as I saw
G               D/F♯
A piece in a jigsaw
A                  Em7
Run up and a - round it
     G                D/F♯
And jump up real tall
A                 Em
Run round the houses
G                 D/F♯
North and the souths'
A                   Em7
You've got your answers
G                 D/F♯
We have both got a sleeping sun
```

Instrumental 4 ‖: A | Asus4 | Asus4 | A :‖

Chorus 2

```
           A     A7sus4
Singing, ooh, ooh, ooh
A     A7sus4
Ooh, ooh, ooh
A     A7sus4
Ooh, ooh, ooh
A     A7sus4
Ooh, ooh, ooh
A    A7sus4
Ah, ah, ah
A    A7sus4
Oh, oh, oh
A    A7sus4
Ah, ah, ah
A    A7sus4
Oh, oh, oh
```

Instrumental 5 | A | A | A | A ‖

‖: A | A | Cadd9 | Cadd9/G :‖

| A7sus4 ‖

SPARKS

Words & Music by
Guy Berryman, Jon Buckland, Will Champion & Chris Martin

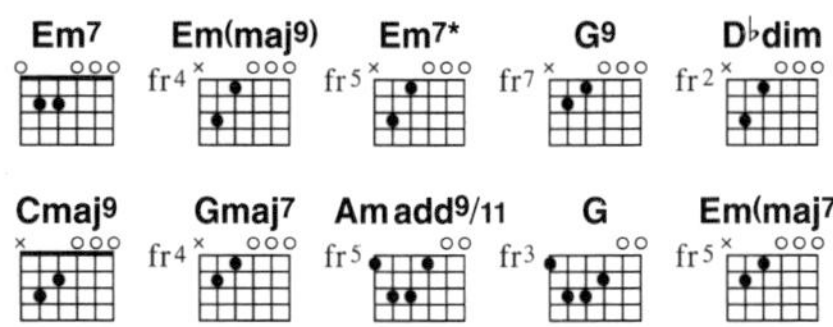

Capo sixth fret, tune guitar (from bottom string): E, A, D, G, B, D

Intro | Em7* Em(maj9) | Em7/G G9 | D♭dim | Cmaj7 |

|: Gmaj7 | Em7* | Gmaj7 | Em7* :|

Verse 1

```
Gmaj7                          Em7*  Gmaj7
   Did I drive you away?
                             Em7*
Well I know what you'll say,
              Am add9/11                  Gmaj7  G  Gmaj7
You'll say "Oh, sing one you know".
                             Em7*  Gmaj7
But I promise you this,
                   Em7     Am add9/11
I'll always look out for you,
                   Gmaj7
That's what I'll do.
```

Bridge 1

```
      Em7  Em(maj9) | Em7*  G9 | D♭dim | Cmaj7 |
Say I, ________________
           Em7  Em(maj9) | Em7*  G9 | D♭dim | Cmaj7 ||
And say I. ________________
```

Link 1 |: Gmaj7 | Em7* | Gmaj7 | Em7* :|

Verse 2

```
Gmaj7                       Em7*   Gmaj7
   My heart is yours,
                 Em7*    Am add9/11
It's you that I hold on to,
                 Gmaj7  G  Gmaj7
That's what I do.
                           Em7*  Em(maj7)  Gmaj7
And I know I was wrong,
                     Em7
But I won't let you down.
Am add9/11                              Gmaj7  G
Oh yeah, I will, yeah I will, yes I will.
```

Bridge 2

```
      Em7  Em(maj9) | Em7*  G9 | D♭dim    | Cmaj7    |
I said I, ________
      Em7  Em(maj9) | Em7*  G9 | D♭dim    | Cmaj7    ||
I cry I. ________
```

Chorus

```
          Gmaj7   Em7*
And I saw sparks,
           Gmaj7   Em7*
Yeah I saw sparks,
      Gmaj7   Em7*
I saw sparks,
           Gmaj7   Em7*
Yeah I saw sparks,
        Gmaj7
See me now.
```

Coda

```
         Em7*  Gmaj7
La la la, la oh,
         Em7*  Gmaj7
La la la, la oh,
         Em7*  Gmaj7
La la la, la oh,
         Em7*  Gmaj7
La la la, la oh.
```

SPIES

Words & Music by
Guy Berryman, Jon Buckland, Will Champion & Chris Martin

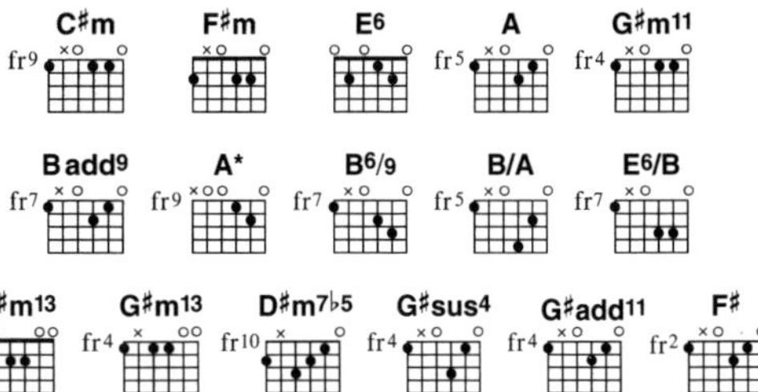

Tune guitar (from bottom string): E, A, C♯, G, B, C♯

Intro | C♯m | C♯m | C♯m | C♯m ||

Verse 1

```
F♯m                           E6
I awake to find no peace of mind,
                A              G♯m11
I said "How do you live as a fugitive?"
          F♯m                       E6
Down here, where I cannot see so clear,
                A
I said "What do I know?"
                 G♯m11
Show me the right way to go.
```

Chorus 1

```
           F♯m                     G♯m11
And the spies came out of the water,
              A                       G♯m11
But you're feeling so bad 'cause you know
           F♯m                     E6
That the spies hide out in every corner,
                              A
But you can't touch them, no,
          Badd9              C♯m    | A*    | B6/9   Badd9 |
'Cause they're all spies
B6/9         Badd9   C♯m   | A*    | B6/9   Badd9 | B6/9   Badd9 ||
They're all spies.
```

Verse 2

F♯m E6
I awake to see that no one is free,
A G♯m11
We're all fugitives, look at the way we live
F♯m E6
Down here, I cannot sleep from fear, no.
A
I said "Which way do I turn?"
G♯m11
Oh, I forget everything I learn.

Chorus 2

As Chorus 1

Bridge

B/A A* E6/B
And if we don't hide here
Badd9 F♯m13
They're going to find us,
G♯m13 F♯m13
If we don't hide now
Badd9 B/A
They're going to catch us where we sleep,
A* E6/B
And if we don't hide here
Badd9 | D♯m7♭5 | G♯sus4 G♯add11 ||
They're going to find us. ________________

Solo

||: C♯m | A* | B6/9 Badd9 | B6/9 Badd9 :||

Chorus 3

A G♯m11
Spies came out of the water,
B/A F♯
And you're feeling so good 'cause you know
F♯m E6
That those spies hide out in every corner
A
And they can't touch you, no,
Badd9
'Cause they're just spies,
B6/9 Badd9 C♯m | A* | B6/9 Badd9 |
They're just spies.

Play 3 times

||: C♯m | A* | B6/9 Badd9 | B6/9 Badd9 :||
They're just spies.

| C♯m ||

SUCH A RUSH

Words & Music by
Guy Berryman, Jon Buckland, Will Champion & Chris Martin

Cm F Cm* Cm6 Cm(maj7) C5
Fm Gm7♭6 G7 B♭ A♭maj7 G7sus4

Intro |: Cm | Cm F | Cm | Cm F :| *Play 3 times*
| Cm | Cm F | Cm | Cm |

Verse 1
Cm* Cm6 Cm(maj7) C5 Cm6 Cm*
Such a rush to do nothing at all,
Cm6 Cm(maj7) C5 Cm6 Fm
Such a fuss to do nothing at all,
Gm7♭6 G7 Cm
Such a rush to do nothing at all.

Verse 2
Cm* Cm6 Cm(maj7) C5 Cm6 Cm*
Such a rush to get nowhere at all,
Cm6 Cm(maj7) C5 Cm6 Fm
Such a fuss to do nothing at all,
Gm7♭6 G7 Cm | Cm F ||
Such a rush. ___________

Chorus 1
Fm B♭
And it's just like you said,
Fm Gm7♭6 G7 Cm
It's just like you said. ___________

Verse 3
Cm* Cm6 Cm(maj7) C5 Cm6 Cm*
Such a rush to do nothing at all,
Cm6 Cm(maj7) C5 Cm6 Fm
Such a fuss to get nowhere at all,
Gm7♭6 G7 | Cm | Cm F ||
Such a rush, such a rush

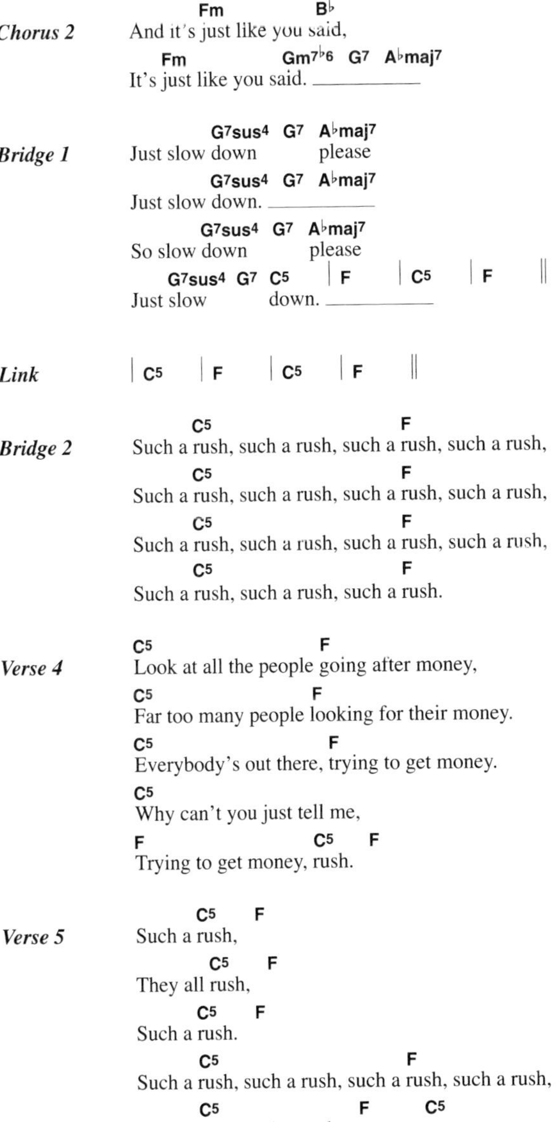

Chorus 2

Fm B♭
And it's just like you said,
Fm Gm7♭6 G7 A♭maj7
It's just like you said. ______

Bridge 1

G7sus4 G7 A♭maj7
Just slow down please
G7sus4 G7 A♭maj7
Just slow down. ______
G7sus4 G7 A♭maj7
So slow down please
G7sus4 G7 C5 | F | C5 | F ||
Just slow down. ______

Link

| C5 | F | C5 | F ||

Bridge 2

C5 F
Such a rush, such a rush, such a rush, such a rush,
C5 F
Such a rush, such a rush, such a rush, such a rush,
C5 F
Such a rush, such a rush, such a rush, such a rush,
C5 F
Such a rush, such a rush, such a rush.

Verse 4

C5 F
Look at all the people going after money,
C5 F
Far too many people looking for their money.
C5 F
Everybody's out there, trying to get money.
C5
Why can't you just tell me,
F C5 F
Trying to get money, rush.

Verse 5

C5 F
Such a rush,
C5 F
They all rush,
C5 F
Such a rush.
C5 F
Such a rush, such a rush, such a rush, such a rush,
C5 F C5
Such a rush, such a rush.

SWALLOWED IN THE SEA

Words & Music by
Guy Berryman, Jon Buckland, Will Champion & Chris Martin

Tune guitar down a semitone

Verse 1

```
      C                G6         Fmaj7              C
You cut me down a tree and brought it back to me,
     G6                   Fmaj7                  C
Well, that's what made me see where I was going wrong.
                        G6          Fmaj7      C
You put me on a shelf and kept me for yourself,
     G6                Fmaj7              C
I can only blame my - self, you can only blame me.
```

Chorus 1

```
      F6                C        Am             G6
And I could write a song, a hundred miles long,
      Fmaj7               C                          G6
Well, that's where I be - long and you belong with me.
      F6                C          Am            G6
And I could write it down and spread it all a - round,
     Fmaj7               C        G6              C
Get lost and then get found, or swallowed in the sea.
```

Verse 2

```
             C        G6       F6               C
You put me on a line and hung me out to dry,
     G6                    Fmaj7        C
And darling, that's when I decide to go to see.
                        G6       F              C
You cut me down to size, and opened up my eyes,
G6               Fmaj7                C
Made me rea - lise what I could not see.
```

Chorus 2

```
      F                C          Am                    G6
And I could write a book, the one they'll say that shook
     Fmaj7              C                         G6
The world and then it took, took it back from me.
      F                 C        Am               G6
And I could write it down, or spread it all a - round,
     Fmaj7              C                                G6
Get lost and then get found and you'll come back to me,
     Fmaj7              C
Not swallowed in the sea.
```

Instrumental ||: Dm Fmaj7 | C G6 | Dm Fmaj7 | C G6 :||

Chorus 3

```
      F                C       Am               G6
And I could write a song, a hundred miles long,
       Fmaj7              C                            G6
Well, that's where I be - long and you belong with me.
      F                           C    Am                 G6
The streets you're walking on, a thousand houses long,
       Fmaj7              C                            G6
Well, that's where I be - long and you belong with me.
            Fmaj7        C            Am            G6
Ah, what good is it to live, with nothing left to give?
       Fmaj7              C                         G6
For - get but not for - give, not loving all you see.
      F                           C    Am                 G6
The streets you're walking on, a thousand houses long,
       Fmaj7              C                            G6
Well, that's where I be - long and you belong with me,
     Fmaj7              C
Not swallowed in the sea.
Am                  G6       F6                   C
You belong with me, not swallowed in the sea,
       Am                  G6       F6                   C
Yeah, you belong with me, not swallowed in the sea.
```

SQUARE ONE

Words & Music by
Guy Berryman, Jon Buckland, Will Champion & Chris Martin

Cm (fr8) F C7sus4 (fr8) E♭6 (fr11) A♭ (fr4)

Fm7 B♭add9(11) F7 E♭ (fr11) Gm (fr3)

Tune guitar (from bottom string): E, A, D, G, C, D♯

Intro | Cm | Cm | Cm | Cm |
| F | F | Cm | Cm ||

Verse 1
Cm C7sus4
You're in control, is there anywhere you want to go?
Cm C7sus4
You're in control, is there anything you want to know?
Cm C7sus4
The future's for dis - covering,
Cm F
The space in which we're travelling.

Instrumental 1 ||: Cm | Cm | F | F :||

Chorus 1
Cm E♭6 A♭
From the top of the first page
Cm E♭6 Fm7
To the end of the last day,
Cm E♭6 A♭
From the start in your own way,
B♭add9(11) A♭
You just want—— somebody listening to what you say,
F7 | F7 | F7 | F7
It doesn't matter who you are.

Instrumental 2 | Cm | Cm | Cm | Cm ||

Verse 2

E♭ Gm Cm
Under the surface trying to break through,—

E♭ Gm Cm
Deciphering the codes in you.—

E♭ Gm Cm
I need a compass, draw me a map,—

E♭ F
I'm on the top, I can't get back.

| Cm | Cm | E♭ | F |

Cm
Whoa, whoa, whoa.

Chorus 2

Cm E♭6 A♭
The first line of the first page

Cm E♭6 Fm7
To the end of the last place, you were looking...

Cm E♭6 A♭
From the start in your own way,

B♭add9(11) A♭
You just want— somebody listening to what you say.

F7
It doesn't matter who you are,

It doesn't matter who you are.

Instrumental 3

𝄆 Cm | E♭6 | A♭ | A♭ |

| Cm | E♭ | Fm7 | Fm7 𝄇

Chorus 3

```
                B♭add9(11)
You just want___
                                        A♭
Somebody listening to what you say,___
                B♭add9(11)                              A♭
You just want___ somebody listening to what you say.
                               F7
It doesn't matter who you are,

It doesn't matter who you are.

|: F7      | F7      | F7      | F7      :|
```

Outro

```
             A♭
Is there anybody out there who
   Fm7
Is lost and hurt and lonely too?
            Cm                                 B♭add9(11)
Are they bleeding all your colours into one?___
                              A♭
And then you come un - done

As if you've been run through,
      Fm7
Some catapult had fired you.
     Cm                                 B♭add9(11)
You wonder if your chance will ever come
                                A♭
Or if you're stuck in square one.
```

TALK

Words & Music by
Guy Berryman, Jon Buckland, Will Champion,
Chris Martin, Ralf Hütter, Karl Bartos & Emil Schult

Gm (fr3) | E♭ (fr6) | B♭ (fr6) | Fsus4 | F | Gm7 (fr3) | Cm (fr3) | E♭maj7 (fr6)

Intro

𝄆 Gm | Gm | Gm | Gm 𝄇
| E♭ | Gm B♭ | E♭ | Gm B♭ |
| E♭ | Gm B♭ | E♭ | Fsus4 F ‖

Verse 1

E♭ Gm B♭ E♭ Gm B♭
Oh, brother I can't, I can't get through,———
E♭ Gm
I've been trying hard to reach you
B♭ E♭ Fsus4 F
'Cos I don't know what to do.———
E♭ Gm B♭ E♭ Gm B♭
Oh, brother I can't be - lieve it's true,———
E♭ Gm
I'm so scared about the future
B♭ E♭ Fsus4 F
And I want to talk to you,———
E♭ Fsus4 F
Oh, I want to talk to you.———

Instrumental 1

| Gm | Gm | Gm | Gm ‖

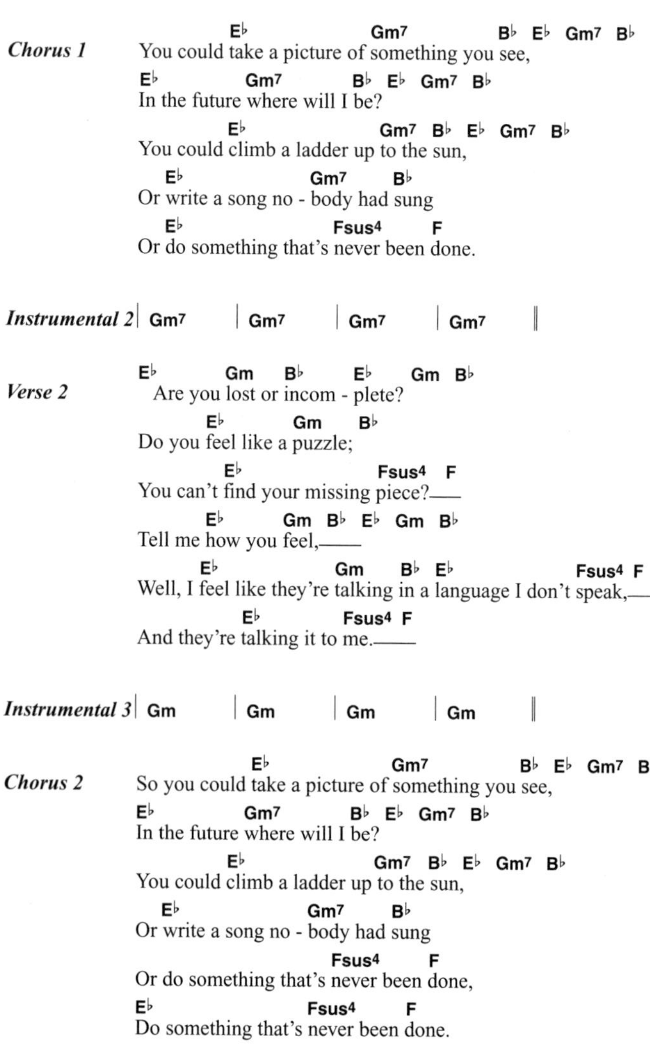

Chorus 1

E♭ Gm7 B♭ E♭ Gm7 B♭
You could take a picture of something you see,
E♭ Gm7 B♭ E♭ Gm7 B♭
In the future where will I be?
E♭ Gm7 B♭ E♭ Gm7 B♭
You could climb a ladder up to the sun,
E♭ Gm7 B♭
Or write a song no - body had sung
E♭ Fsus4 F
Or do something that's never been done.

Instrumental 2 | Gm7 | Gm7 | Gm7 | Gm7 ||

Verse 2

E♭ Gm B♭ E♭ Gm B♭
Are you lost or incom - plete?
E♭ Gm B♭
Do you feel like a puzzle;
E♭ Fsus4 F
You can't find your missing piece?___
E♭ Gm B♭ E♭ Gm B♭
Tell me how you feel,___
E♭ Gm B♭ E♭ Fsus4 F
Well, I feel like they're talking in a language I don't speak,___
E♭ Fsus4 F
And they're talking it to me.___

Instrumental 3 | Gm | Gm | Gm | Gm ||

Chorus 2

E♭ Gm7 B♭ E♭ Gm7 B♭
So you could take a picture of something you see,
E♭ Gm7 B♭ E♭ Gm7 B♭
In the future where will I be?
E♭ Gm7 B♭ E♭ Gm7 B♭
You could climb a ladder up to the sun,
E♭ Gm7 B♭
Or write a song no - body had sung
Fsus4 F
Or do something that's never been done,
E♭ Fsus4 F
Do something that's never been done.

Instrumental 4 | Gm7 | Gm7 | Gm7 | Gm7 |

|: Cm | E♭ | Gm | F |

| Cm | E♭ | Gm | F :|

Guitar solo | E♭ | Gm B♭ | E♭ | Gm B♭ |

| E♭ | Gm B♭ | E♭ | Fsus4 F ||

Chorus 3

```
            E♭
So you don't know where you're going
              Gm7     B♭  E♭  Gm7  B♭
And you want to talk,
    E♭
You feel like you're going
                      Gm7       B♭  E♭  Gm7  B♭
Where you've been be - fore,
              E♭
You'll tell anyone who'll listen
             Gm7     B♭  E♭  Gm7  B♭
But you feel ig - nored,
     E♭                                    Gm7     B♭
And nothing's really making any sense at all.
     E♭        F
Let's talk, let's talk,
      E♭maj7    F     Gm
Let's talk, let's talk.
```

THINGS I DON'T UNDERSTAND

Words & Music by
Guy Berryman, Jon Buckland, Will Champion & Chris Martin

C Em Am F G Dm G6

```
Intro      |: C      | Em     | Am     | Em     |
           | F       | G      | Am     | Am    :|
           | F       | G      | Am     | Am     ||
```

```
                C                 Em        Am                 Em
Verse 1    How tides control the sea, and what becomes of me
                F               G                  Am
           How little things can slip out of your hands.
                C            Em          Am              Em
           How often people change, no two remain the same
                F                   G              Am
           Why things don't always turn out as you plan.
           F                    G              Am
           These are things that I don't under - stand
                 F                   G              Am
           Yeah, these are things that I don't under - stand.
```

```
             Dm                     G
Chorus 1   I can't, and I can't de - cide
           Am                        F
           Wrong, all my wrong from right.
           Dm                 G
           Day, all my day for night
           Am                   F
           Dark, all my dark for light
             Dm                G
           I live, but I love this life.

           | Am     | Am     | G6     | G6     ||
```

Link 1

```
| C      | Em     | Am     | Em     |
| F      | G      | Am     | Am     |
| F      | G      | Am     | Am     ||
```

Verse 2

```
    C           Em         Am               Em
How infinite is space, and who decides your fate
    F                G            Am
Why everything will dissolve into sand.
       C          Em          Am                Em
How to avoid de - feat, where truth and fiction meet
    F             G                 Am
Why nothing ever turns out as you planned.
F                       G             Am
These are things that I don't under - stand
      F                       G             Am
Yeah, these are things that I don't under - stand.
```

Chorus 2

```
  Dm                      G
I can't, and I can't de - cide
Am                       F
Wrong, all my wrong from right
Dm                  G
Day, all my day for night.
Am                    F
Dark, all my dark for light
  Dm                    G
I live, but I love this life.
```

```
| F      | F      | F      | F      ||
  let ring...
```

Outro

```
||: C    | Em     | Am     | Em     |
| F      | G      | Am     | Am     :||
||: F    | G      | Am     | Am     :||
| F      | G      | Am     | Am     ||
                    let ring...
```

TIL KINGDOM COME

Words & Music by
Guy Berryman, Jon Buckland, Will Champion & Chris Martin

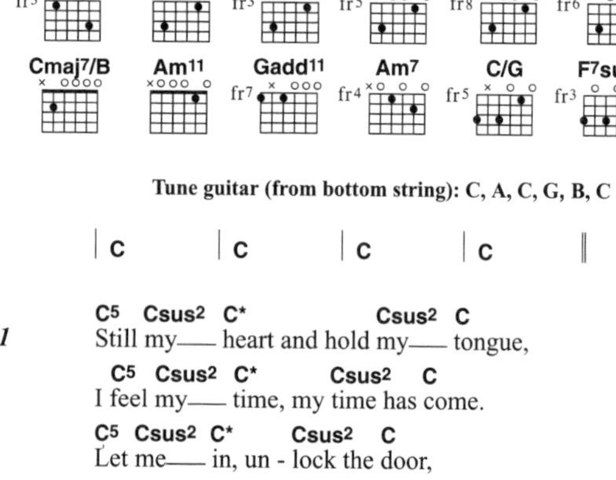

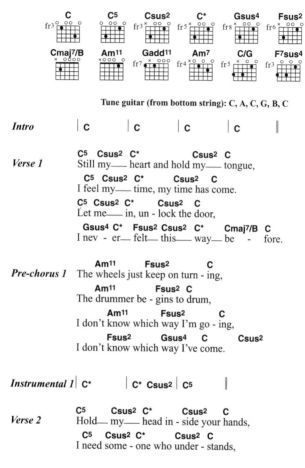

Tune guitar (from bottom string): C, A, C, G, B, C

Intro | C | C | C | C ||

Verse 1
C5 Csus2 C* Csus2 C
Still my— heart and hold my— tongue,
C5 Csus2 C* Csus2 C
I feel my— time, my time has come.
C5 Csus2 C* Csus2 C
Let me— in, un - lock the door,
Gsus4 C* Fsus2 Csus2 C* Cmaj7/B C
I nev - er— felt— this— way— be - fore.

Pre-chorus 1
Am11 Fsus2 C
The wheels just keep on turn - ing,
Am11 Fsus2 C
The drummer be - gins to drum,
Am11 Fsus2 C
I don't know which way I'm go - ing,
Fsus2 Gsus4 C Csus2
I don't know which way I've come.

Instrumental 1 | C* | C* Csus2 | C5 ||

Verse 2
C5 Csus2 C* Csus2 C
Hold— my— head in - side your hands,
C5 Csus2 C* Csus2 C
I need some - one who under - stands,

cont.

C5 Csus2 C* Csus2 C
I need some - one; some - one who hears,
Gsus4 C* Fsus2 Csus2 C* Cmaj7/B C
For you— I've wait - ed—— all these—— years.

Chorus 1

Fsus2 C
For you I'd wait til kingdom come,
Fsus2 C
Until my day, my day is done.
Fsus2 Gadd11 Am7
Say you'll come and set me— free,
C/G F7sus4 C Csus2
Just say you'll wait,——— you'll wait for me.

Instrumental 2 | C* | C* Csus2 | C5 ||

Verse 3

C5 Csus2 C* Csus2 C
In— your— tears and in your blood,
C5 Csus2 C* Csus2 C
In— your– fire and in your flood,
C5 Csus2 C* Csus2 C
I heard you—— laugh, I heard you sing,
Gsus4 C* Fsus2 Csus2 C* Cmaj7/B C
I would - n't— change a——— sin - gle——— thing.

Pre-chorus 2

Am11 Fsus2 C
The wheels just keep on turn - ing,
Am11 Fsus2 C
The drummers be - gin to drum.
Am11 Fsus2 C
I don't know which way I'm go - ing,
Fsus2 Gsus4 C
I don't know which way I've come.

Chorus 2

Fsus2 C
For you I'd wait til kingdom come,
Fsus2 C
Until my days, my days are done.
Fsus2 Gadd11 Am7
Say you'll come and set me— free,
C/G F7sus4 C
Just say you'll wait,——— you'll wait for me.
C/G F7sus4 C
Just say you'll wait,——— you'll wait for me.
C/G F7sus4 C
Just say you'll wait,——— you'll wait for me.

TROUBLE

Words & Music by
Guy Berryman, Jon Buckland, Will Champion & Chris Martin

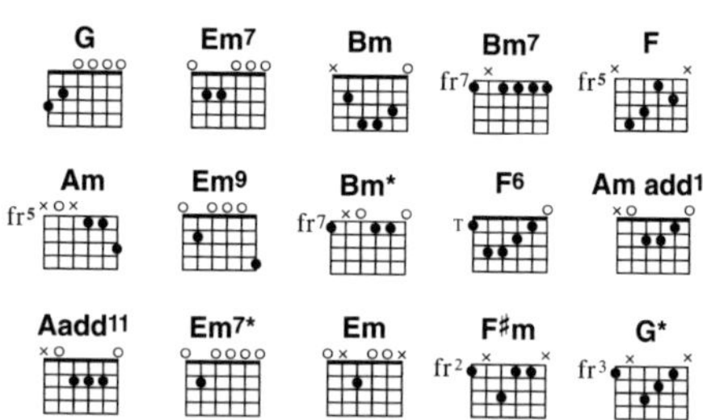

Tune guitar (from bottom string): E, A, D, G, B, D

Intro ‖: G Em7 | Bm | G Em7 | Bm :‖

Verse 1

G Em7 Bm7
Oh no, I see,
F Am G
A spider web is tangled up with me,
Em7 Bm7
And I lost my head,
F Am G
And thought of all the stupid things I'd said.

Link 1 | G Em7 | Bm | G Em7 | Bm ‖

Verse 2

G Em9 Bm*
Oh no, what's this?
F6 Am add11
A spider web, and I'm caught in the middle,
G Em9 Bm*
So I turn to run,
F6 Am add11 G
And thought of all the stupid things I'd done.

Chorus 1

Aadd11 Em7
And ah, I never meant to cause you trouble,
Aadd11 Em7
And ah, I never meant to do you wrong,
Aadd11 Em7
And ah, well if I ever caused you trouble,
Aadd11 Em7
Then oh, I never meant to do you harm.

Link 2

| G Em7 | Bm | G Em7 | Bm ||

Verse 3

G Em9 Bm*
Oh no, I see,
F6 Am add11
A spider web and it's me in the middle,
G Em7 Bm*
So I twist and turn,
F6 Am add11 G
But here I am in my little bubble.

Chorus 2

Aadd11 Em7
Singing out ah, I never meant to cause you trouble,
Aadd11 Em7
And ah, I never meant to do you wrong,
Aadd11 Em7
And ah, well if I ever caused you trouble,
Aadd11 Em7
Then oh no I never meant to do you harm.

Link 3

|: G Em9 | Bm* | G Em9 | Bm* :|

Coda

Em F♯m G* F♯m Em
And they spun a web for me,
F♯m G* F♯m Em
And they spun a web for me,
F♯m G* F♯m Em | Em |
And they spun a web for me.

|: G Em7 | Bm* | G Em7 | Bm* :|

TWISTED LOGIC

Words & Music by
Guy Berryman, Jon Buckland, Will Champion & Chris Martin

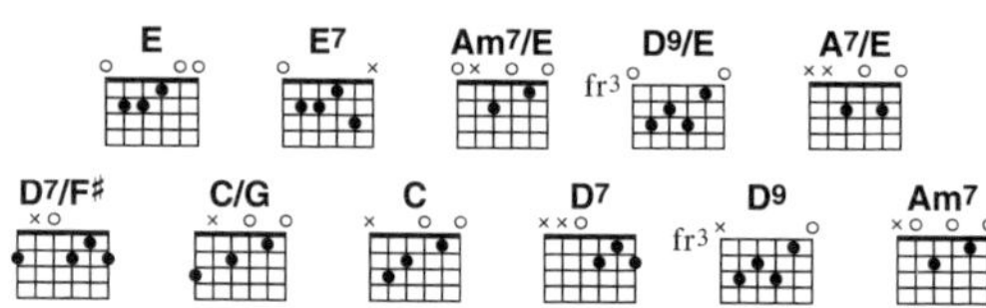

Tune guitar down a semitone

Verse 1

E E7 Am7/E
Sunlight— opened up my eyes,

D9/E E E7
To see for the first time

Am7/E D9/E
It opened them up,

E E7 Am7/E D9/E
And tonight,— rivers will run dry,

E E7 A7/E D9/E
And not for the first time,— rivers will run.

Instrumental 1 ‖: D7/F# | C/G | C | D7 :‖

Verse 2

E E7 Am7/E D9/E
Hundreds— of years in the future

E E7
There could be com - puters

Am7/E D9/E E
Looking for life— on— Earth,

E7 Am7/E D9/E
So don't fight for the wrong side,

E E7
Say what you feel like,

A7/E D9/E
Say how you feel.———

Instrumental 2 | C | D9 | E | Am7 |

| C | D9 | E | Am7 ‖

Chorus 1

C D9
You'll go backwards a - gain,
E Am7
You'll go forwards a - gain,
C D9
You'll go backwards a - gain, you'll go.

Instrumental 3 ‖: E | E7 | Am7/E | D9/E :‖

Verse 3

E E7 Am7/E D9/E
Creat - ed— then drilled and in - vaded,
E E7
If somebody made it,
Am7/E D9/E E
Someone will mess— it— up.
E7 Am7/E D9/E
And you are not wrong to
E E7
Ask, "Who does this be - long to?"
Am7/E D9/E
It belongs to all— of us.

Instrumental 4 ‖: D7/F♯ | C/G | C | D7 :‖ E | E ‖

Chorus 2

C D9
You'll go backwards a - gain,
E Am7
You'll go forwards a - gain,
C D9
You'll go backwards a - gain,
E
You'll go forwards.
C D9
You'll go backwards a - gain,
E Am7
You'll go forwards a - gain,
C D9
You'll go backwards a - gain,
E
You'll go forwards.

Instrumental 5 | C | D9 | E | Am7 |
| C | D9 | E (fermata) ‖

WARNING SIGN

Words & Music by
Guy Berryman, Jon Buckland, Will Champion & Chris Martin

Dadd9 G D A E Esus4

F♯m Em/G E/G♯ Gmaj7 F♯m7 Em7/A Dmaj7/F♯

Capo first fret

Intro | Dadd9 | Dadd9 | Dadd9 | Dadd9 |

|: G D | A E | G D | A E :|

Verse 1
```
G           D
A warning sign,
A         Esus4  E                    G         D
  I missed the good part then I realised,
A         Esus4  E             G         D
  I started looking and the bubble burst,
A         Esus4  E          G       D       A       Esus4
  I started looking for excuses.
```

Verse 2
```
G        D
Come on in,
A          Esus4  E             G          D
  I've got to tell you what a state I'm in.
A               Esus4 E         G          D
  I've got to tell you in my loudest tones
A               Esus4    E         G          D
  That I started looking for a warning sign.
```

| A Esus4 E | E |

Chorus 1
```
             D          F♯m
When the truth is
      A     E/G♯
I miss you.
             D          F♯m
Yeah, the truth is
             A          E/G♯
That I miss you so.
```

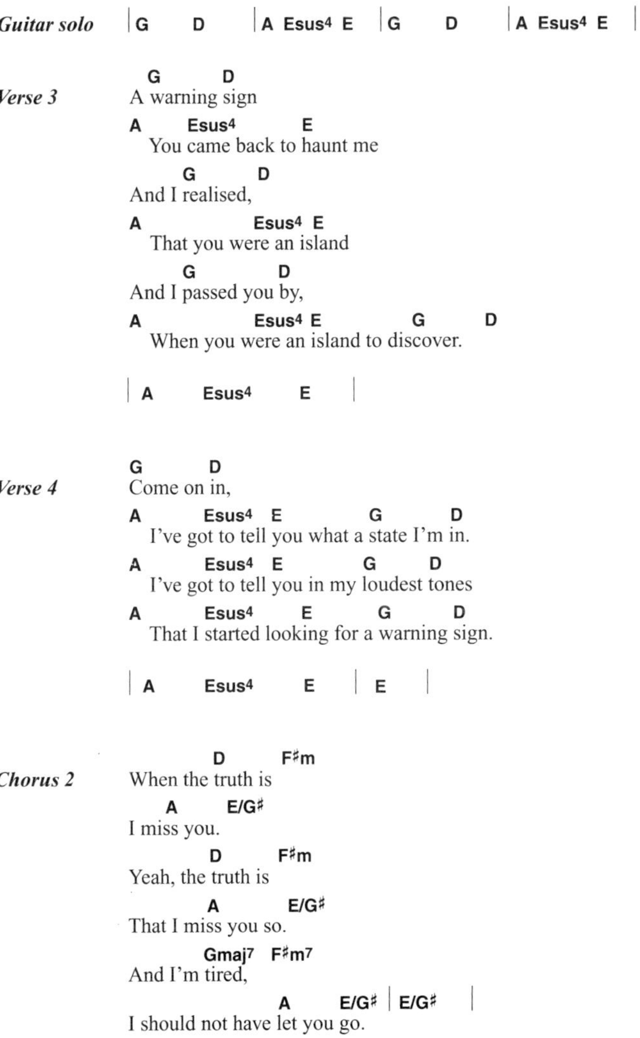

Guitar solo | G D | A Esus4 E | G D | A Esus4 E |

Verse 3

G D
A warning sign
A Esus4 E
You came back to haunt me
G D
And I realised,
A Esus4 E
That you were an island
G D
And I passed you by,
A Esus4 E G D
When you were an island to discover.

| A Esus4 E |

Verse 4

G D
Come on in,
A Esus4 E G D
I've got to tell you what a state I'm in.
A Esus4 E G D
I've got to tell you in my loudest tones
A Esus4 E G D
That I started looking for a warning sign.

| A Esus4 E | E |

Chorus 2

D F♯m
When the truth is
A E/G♯
I miss you.
D F♯m
Yeah, the truth is
A E/G♯
That I miss you so.
Gmaj7 F♯m7
And I'm tired,
A E/G♯ | E/G♯ |
I should not have let you go.

```
Middle      | A         | Em7/A     | G         | Dmaj7/F#  |
              Oh.

            | A         | Em7/A     | G         | Dmaj7/F#  |

                  A       Em7/A          G             Dmaj7/F#
Outro       So I crawl back into your open arms.
                   A       Em7/A          G            Dmaj7/F#
            Yes I crawl back into your open arms.
                   A       Em7/A          G            Dmaj7/F#
            And I crawl back into your open arms.
                   A       Em7/A                       F#m (fermata)
            Yes I crawl back into your open arms.
```

WHITE SHADOWS

Words & Music by
Guy Berryman, Jon Buckland, Will Champion & Chris Martin

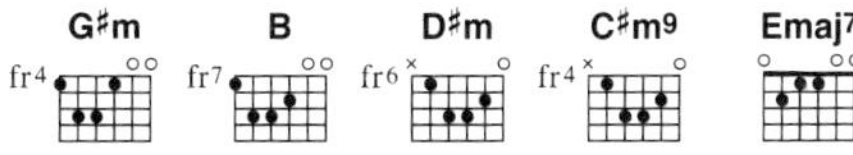

Tune top string to D♯

Intro | G♯m | G♯m |: G♯m | B | D♯m | C♯m9 :|

Verse 1
G♯m B
When I was a young boy
D♯m C♯m9
I tried to listen
G♯m B D♯m
And I want to feel like that...
G♯m B D♯m C♯m9
Little white shadows, blink and miss them,
G♯m B D♯m
Part of a system I am.

Instrumental 1 | G♯m | G♯m | D♯m | C♯m9 |
| G♯m | G♯m | D♯m | D♯m ||

Verse 2
G♯m B D♯m C♯m9
If you ever feel like something's missing,
G♯m B D♯m
Things you never under - stand,
G♯m B D♯m C♯m9
Little white shadows sparkle and glis - ten,
G♯m B D♯m
Part of a system, a plan.

Pre-chorus1

```
Emaj7                 C#m9
  All this noise I'm waking up,
Emaj7                 C#m9
  All the space I'm taking up,
Emaj7                C#m9
  All this sound is breaking up,
Emaj7           C#m9
  Whoa, whoa.______
```

Chorus1

```
G#m                             Emaj7
Maybe you'll get what you wanted,
B                               D#m
Maybe you'll stumble up - on it.
G#m                     Emaj7         B              D#m
Everything you ever wanted, in a permanent state,
G#m                                   Emaj7
Maybe you'll know when you've seen it,
B                              D#m
Maybe if you say it you'll mean it,
G#m                              Emaj7
And when you find it you'll keep it
     B                  D#m                      (G#m)
In a permanent state,    a permanent state.
```

Instrumental 2

```
| G#m    | G#m    | D#m    | C#m9    |
(state.)
| G#m    | G#m    | D#m    | C#m9    ||
```

Verse3

```
G#m                 B
  When I was a young boy
  D#m           C#m9
  I tried to lis - ten,
G#m                      B         D#m
  Don't you want to feel like that?
G#m                      B
  You're part of the human race,
D#m                               C#m9
  All of the stars and the outer space...
G#m          B          D#m
  Part of a system I am.
```

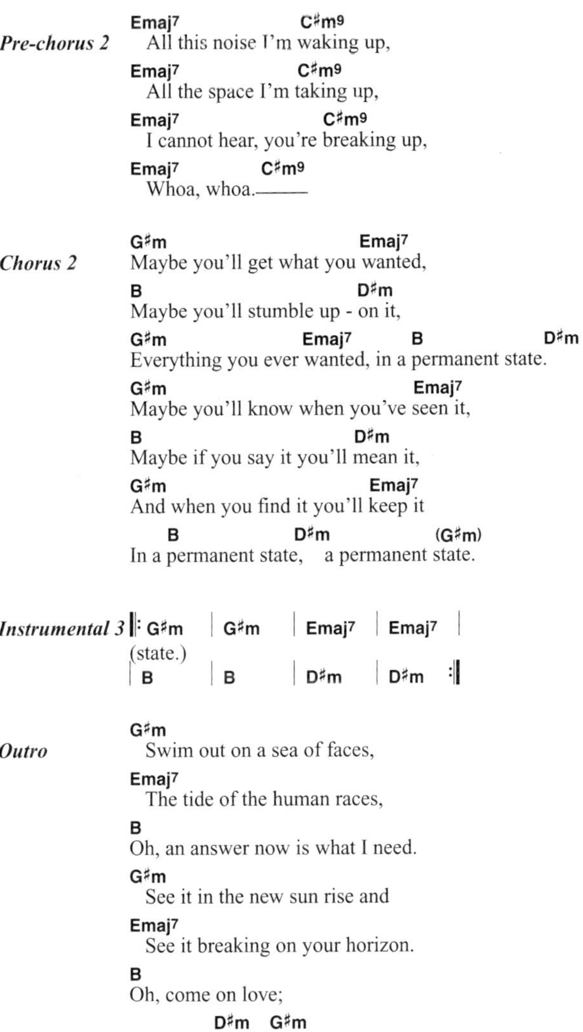

Pre-chorus 2

Emaj7 C♯m9
All this noise I'm waking up,

Emaj7 C♯m9
All the space I'm taking up,

Emaj7 C♯m9
I cannot hear, you're breaking up,

Emaj7 C♯m9
Whoa, whoa.___

Chorus 2

G♯m Emaj7
Maybe you'll get what you wanted,

B D♯m
Maybe you'll stumble up - on it,

G♯m Emaj7 B D♯m
Everything you ever wanted, in a permanent state.

G♯m Emaj7
Maybe you'll know when you've seen it,

B D♯m
Maybe if you say it you'll mean it,

G♯m Emaj7
And when you find it you'll keep it

B D♯m (G♯m)
In a permanent state, a permanent state.

Instrumental 3

‖: G♯m | G♯m | Emaj7 | Emaj7 |
(state.)
| B | B | D♯m | D♯m :‖

Outro

G♯m
Swim out on a sea of faces,

Emaj7
The tide of the human races,

B
Oh, an answer now is what I need.

G♯m
See it in the new sun rise and

Emaj7
See it breaking on your horizon.

B
Oh, come on love;

D♯m G♯m
Stay with me.___

WE NEVER CHANGE

Words & Music by
Guy Berryman, Jon Buckland, Will Champion & Chris Martin

F♯madd11 E6 Bmadd9 Aadd9 C♯m7

Bm9 B7sus2 Bmadd9* F♯m Dmaj7 Badd9

Tune guitar (from bottom string): E, A, D, G, B, C♯

Intro ||: F♯madd11 | F♯madd11 | E6 | E6 :||

Verse 1

```
                  F♯madd11              E6
I wanna live life and never be cruel,
                        F♯madd11              E6
And I wanna live life and be good to you,
          Bmadd9   F♯madd11              E6
And I wanna   fly and never come down,
        Bmadd9  F♯madd11                E6        Aadd9
And live my   life and have friends around.
```

Chorus 1

```
                                   C♯m7         Aadd9
But we never change, do we? No, no,
                          C♯m7
We never learn, do we?
       Bmadd9   F♯madd11          E6
So I wanna   live in a wooden house.
```

Verse 2

```
                  F♯madd11              E6
I wanna live life and always be true,
                  F♯madd11              E6
I wanna live life and be good to you,
Bmadd9    F♯madd11              E6
I wanna   fly and never come down,
        Bmadd9  F♯madd11                E6        Aadd9
And live my   life and have friends around.
```

Chorus 2

C♯m7 Aadd9
But we never change, do we? No, no,

C♯m7
We never learn, do we?

Bmadd9 F♯madd11 E6
So I wanna live in a wooden house,

Bmadd9 F♯madd11 E6
Where making more friends would be easy.

Bridge

Bm9 B7sus2 Bm9 B7sus2 E6 Bm9
Oh, I don't have a soul to save,

B7sus2 Bm9 B7sus2 E6 Bmadd9
Yes, and I sin every single day.

Chorus 3

F♯madd11 E6 Bmadd9
We never change, do we?

F♯madd11 E6
We never learn, do we?

Outro

Bmadd9 F♯m E6 Bmadd9*
So I wanna live in a wooden house,

F♯m Dmaj7 Badd9
Where making more friends would be ea - sy.

Bmadd9 F♯m E6 Bmadd9
I wanna live where the sun comes out.

WHAT IF

Words & Music by
Guy Berryman, Jon Buckland, Will Champion & Chris Martin

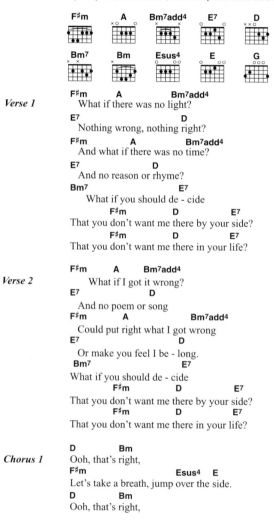

F♯m A Bm7add4 E7 D
Bm7 Bm Esus4 E G

Verse 1

```
F♯m        A             Bm7add4
   What if there was no light?
E7                         D
   Nothing wrong, nothing right?
F♯m           A             Bm7add4
   And what if there was no time?
E7                   D
   And no reason or rhyme?
Bm7                            E7
     What if you should de - cide
             F♯m                D              E7
That you don't want me there by your side?
             F♯m                D             E7
That you don't want me there in your life?
```

Verse 2

```
F♯m          A          Bm7add4
     What if I got it wrong?
E7                    D
   And no poem or song
F♯m             A                  Bm7add4
   Could put right what I got wrong
E7                             D
   Or make you feel I be - long.
 Bm7                           E7
What if you should de - cide
              F♯m               D              E7
That you don't want me there by your side?
              F♯m               D              E7
That you don't want me there in your life?
```

Chorus 1

```
D             Bm
Ooh, that's right,
F♯m                              Esus4    E
Let's take a breath, jump over the side.
D             Bm
Ooh, that's right,
```

cont.

F♯m   Esus4   E
How can you know it when you don't even try?
D   Bm
Ooh, that's right.

Verse 3

F♯m   A   Bm7add4
  Every step that you take
E7   D
  Could be your biggest mis - take,
F♯m   A   Bm7add4
  It could bend or it could break
E7   D
  But that's the risk that you take.
Bm7   E7
    What if you should de - cide
            F♯m   D   E7
That you don't want me there in your life?
            F♯m   D   E7
That you don't want me there by your side?

Chorus 2

D   Bm
Ooh, that's right,
F♯m   Esus4   E
Let's take a breath, jump over the side,
D   Bm
Ooh, that's right.
F♯m   Esus4   E
How can you know it when you don't even try?
G   D   E
Ooh, that's right.

Chorus 3

D   Bm
Ooh, that's right,
F♯m   Esus4   E
Let's take a breath, jump over the side,
D   Bm
Ooh, that's right.
F♯m   Esus4   E
You know that darkness always turns into light,
G   D   E
Ooh, that's right.

A WHISPER

Words & Music by
Guy Berryman, Jon Buckland, Will Champion & Chris Martin

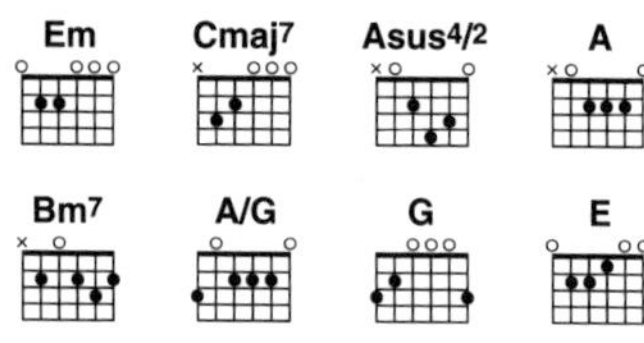

Capo third fret

Intro |: Em | Em | Em | Em :|

Chorus 1
```
Cmaj7                                        Em
   A whisper, a whisper, a whisper, a whisper.
Cmaj7                                       (Em)
   A whisper, a whisper, a whisper, a whisper.
```

Link 1 | Em | Em | Em | Em ||

Verse 1
```
Asus4/2    A              Asus4/2   A
I hear the sound of the ticking of clocks,
      Asus4/2           A
Who remembers your face,
      Asus4/2          A              Em
Who remembers you when you are (gone?)
```

Link 2 | Em | Em | Em | Em ||
gone?

Verse 2
```
Asus4/2    A              Asus4/2   A
I hear the sound of the ticking of clocks
Asus4/2          A
Come back and look for me,
Asus4/2       A         Em
Look for me when I am lost.
```

Chorus 2
```
               Cmaj7                                   Em
And just a whisper, a whisper, a whisper, a whisper.
          Cmaj7                                (Em)
Just a whisper, a whisper, a whisper, a whisper.
```

Link 3 | Em | Em | Em | Em ||

Middle

Bm7 Cmaj7 A
Night turns to day, and I still have these questions,
Bm7 Cmaj7 A
Bridges will break, should I go forwards or backwards?
Bm7 Cmaj7 A A/G
And night turns to day, and I still get no answers.

| Em | Em |

Chorus 3

Cmaj7 Em
A whisper, a whisper, a whisper, a whisper.
Cmaj7 Em
Just a whisper, a whisper, a whisper, a whisper.

Link 4 | Em | Em | Em |

Verse 3

Asus4/2 A Asus4/2 A
I hear the sound of the ticking of clocks,
Asus4/2 A
Who remembers your face,
Asus4/2 A Em | Em |
Who remembers you when you are gone?

Verse 4

Asus4/2 A Asus4/2 A
I hear the sound of the ticking of clocks
Asus4/2 A
Come back and look for me,
Asus4/2 A Em
Look for me when I am lost.

Chorus 4

Cmaj7 Em
And just a whisper, a whisper, a whisper, a whisper.
Cmaj7
Just a whisper, a whisper, a whisper, a whisper.

Link 4 | E | E | E | E ||

Outro ||: G A | E | G A | E |
| G A | E | G A | E :|| *Repeat to fade*

Words & Music by
Guy Berryman, Jon Buckland, Will Champion & Chris Martin

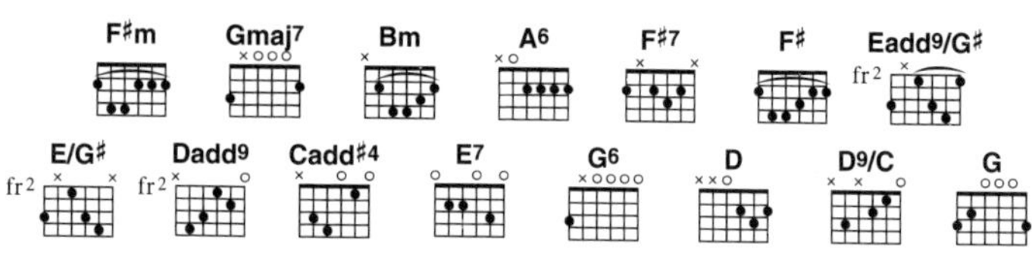

Verse 1

F#m Gmaj7
Trying hard to speak and
Bm A6
Fighting with my weak hand.
F#m Gmaj7
Driven to dis - traction
Bm A6
It's all part of the plan.
F#7 Gmaj7
When something is broken
Bm A6
And you try and fix it,
F#m Gmaj7
Trying to re - pair it
Eadd9/G# Gmaj7
Any way you can.

Instrumental 1 | Eadd9/G# | Gmaj7 | Eadd9/G# | Gmaj7 ||

Verse 2

F#m Gmaj7
I dive in at the deep end,
Bm A6
You become my best friend.
F#m Gmaj7 Bm A6
I want to love you but I don't know if I can,
F#7 Gmaj7
I know something is broken
Bm A6
And I'm trying to fix it.

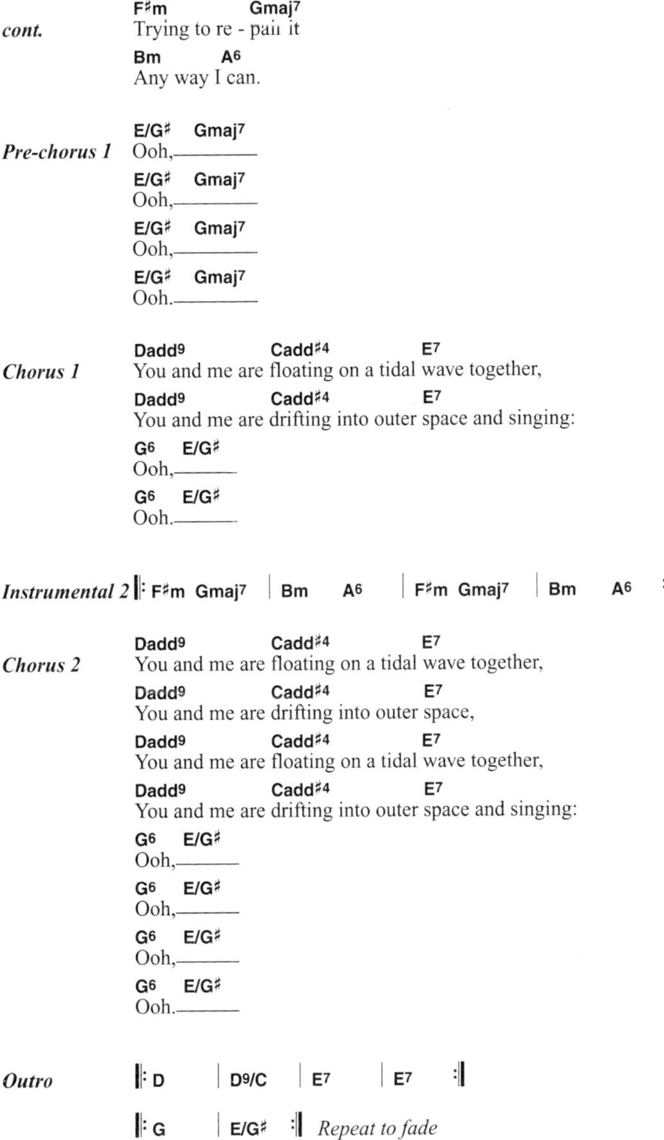

cont.

F♯m Gmaj7
Trying to re - pair it
Bm A6
Any way I can.

Pre-chorus 1

E/G♯ Gmaj7
Ooh,________
E/G♯ Gmaj7
Ooh,________
E/G♯ Gmaj7
Ooh,________
E/G♯ Gmaj7
Ooh.________

Chorus 1

Dadd9 Cadd♯4 E7
You and me are floating on a tidal wave together,
Dadd9 Cadd♯4 E7
You and me are drifting into outer space and singing:
G6 E/G♯
Ooh,______
G6 E/G♯
Ooh.______

Instrumental 2 ‖: F♯m Gmaj7 | Bm A6 | F♯m Gmaj7 | Bm A6 :‖

Chorus 2

Dadd9 Cadd♯4 E7
You and me are floating on a tidal wave together,
Dadd9 Cadd♯4 E7
You and me are drifting into outer space,
Dadd9 Cadd♯4 E7
You and me are floating on a tidal wave together,
Dadd9 Cadd♯4 E7
You and me are drifting into outer space and singing:
G6 E/G♯
Ooh,______
G6 E/G♯
Ooh,______
G6 E/G♯
Ooh,______
G6 E/G♯
Ooh.______

Outro ‖: D | D9/C | E7 | E7 :‖

‖: G | E/G♯ :‖ *Repeat to fade*

YELLOW

Words & Music by
Guy Berryman, Jon Buckland, Will Champion & Chris Martin

B   Badd11   F#6   Emaj7

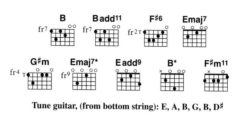

G#m   Emaj7*   Eadd9   B*   F#m11

Tune guitar, (from bottom string): E, A, B, G, B, D#

Intro

| B | B Badd11 | B | B Badd11 || B | B add11 |

| F#6 | F#6 | Emaj7 | Emaj7 | B | B add11 ||

Verse 1

```
B                                         F#6
   Look at the stars, look how they shine for  you
                       Emaj7
And everything  you do,

Yeah, they were all yellow.
B                                   F#6
   I came along, I wrote a song for  you
                         Emaj7
And all the things you do,

And it was called yellow.
B       Badd11          F#6
   So then I took my __ turn,
                              Emaj7
Oh what a thing to've done
                         B   Badd11 B
And it was all yellow.
```

Chorus 1

```
Emaj7       G#m        F#6
   Your skin,  oh yeah, your  skin and bones
Emaj7*  G#m      F#6
   Turn into something beautiful,
Emaj7            G#m             F#6          Emaj7
   And you know,   you know I love you so,
Eadd9
   You know I love you so.
```

Link 1 | B | B | F♯6 | F♯6 |

| Emaj7 | Emaj7 | B | B ||

Verse 2
B F♯6
I swam across, I jumped across for you,
Emaj7
Oh, what a thing to do
'Cause you were all yellow.
B Badd11 F♯6
I drew a line, I drew a line for you,
Emaj7
Oh, what a thing to do
B Badd11 B
And it was all yellow.

Chorus 2
Emaj7 G♯m F♯6
Your skin, oh yeah, your skin and bones
Emaj7* G♯m F♯6
Turn into something beautiful,
Emaj7 G♯m F♯6 Emaj7
And you know? For you I bleed myself dry,
Eadd9
For you I bleed myself (dry.)

Link 2 | B | B | F♯6 | F♯6 |
dry.

| Emaj7 | Emaj7 | B | B ||

Coda
B F♯6
It's true, look how they shine for you,
Emaj7
Look how they shine for you, look how they shine for,
B F♯6
Look how they shine for you,
Emaj7
Look how they shine for you, look how they shine.
B*
Look at the stars,
F♯madd11
Look how they shine for you
Emaj7
And all the things that you __ do.

THE WORLD TURNED UPSIDE DOWN

Words & Music by
Guy Berryman, Jon Buckland, Will Champion & Chris Martin

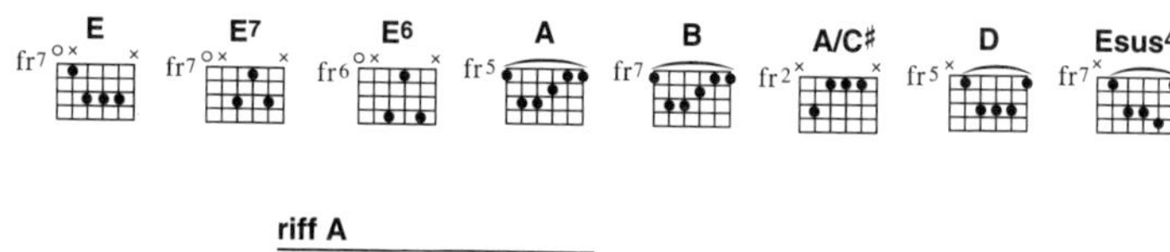

riff A
E E7 E6 E7
Intro X and Y
riff A
The land, sea, rivers, trees, the stars, the sky
riff A
That and this
riff A
We're part of a bigger plan.
riff A
Don't know what it is,

Don't know what it is.

Link 1 𝄆 E | E | E | E 𝄇

riff A
Verse 1 You and me
riff A
The land, sun, trees, the sky, the stars, the sea
riff A
365 Degrees

I am a puzzle, you're the missing piece.
riff A
Hang on a minute, just a minute please

I'll come
riff A
And everything under the sun,

And everything under the sun.

Chorus 1

A   B
What is this feeling that I can't explain
        A/C$^{\sharp}$ D
And why am I never gonna sleep again.
A   B
    What is this thing I've never seen before
    A/C$^{\sharp}$ D
A little boy lost in a breaking storm.
A   B
Hide and sob, and away they fly
      A/C$^{\sharp}$ D
To write your name in the summer sky.
A   B
    Life has really only just begun
A/C$^{\sharp}$
Life that comes
        D*
And everything under the sun.

Link 2

𝄆 E | E | E | E 𝄇

Verse 2

riff A
X is Y
riff A
The land, sea, rivers, trees, the stars, the sky
riff A
365 Degrees

All of the surface and the underneath.
riff A
Searching your mellow and outsings your key, ah

                                                                riff A
And everything under the sun,

And everything under the sun.

Chorus 2

A B
What is this feeling that I can't explain
A/C♯ D
And why am I never gonna sleep again
A B
What is this thing I've never seen before
A/C♯ D
A little boy lost in a breaking storm
A B
Hide and sob, and away they fly
A/C♯ D
To write your name in the summer sky
A B
Life has really only just begun
A/C♯
Life that comes
D*
And everything under the sun

Link 3

𝄆 N.C. | N.C. | N.C. | N.C. 𝄇

Bridge

B Esus4 E
And you don't know that you've been born
B Esus4 E
Can't see the calm until the storm
B Esus4 E
Can't tell your right side from your wrong
B Esus4 E
Can't see the wave you're riding on

Outro

𝄆 E | E | E | E 𝄇

1 2 3 4 5 6 7 8 9